Go to 197 or your gay!!

The **100** Most Beautiful Treasures of Russia

A cultural journey through Russian history

REBO
PUBLISHERS

© 2008 Rebo International b.v., Lisse, the Netherlands

Concept: Tobias Pehle
Authors: Thomas Veser, Silvia Jonas, Martina Handwerker
Graphic design: Medien Kommunikation, Unna, Germany
Project editors: Yara Hackstein (editor in chief), Lena Djattschina, Henning Mohr, Clarissa Conrad, Sabine Ringel, Raphael Pehle, Peter Richter
Typesetting: A.R. Garamond, Prague, Czech Republic
Translator: Susan Ghanouni in association with First Edition Translations Ltd., Cambridge, UK
Editor: Lin Thomas in association with First Edition Translations Ltd., Cambridge, UK
Proofreading: Sarah Dunham, Erin Ferretti Slattery

ISBN 978 90 366 2348 3

Foreword

Dear Reader,

Russia is unbelievably vast and rich in impressive cultural treasures, historical sites and fascinating architectural monuments left behind by the Grand Princes of the Kievan Rus in the 9th century, the Tatars in the 13th and 14th centuries, and the Soviets in the 20th century, for example. It is undoubtedly the Tsars to whom we are indebted for the most shining examples of Russia's cultural history. Not only were countless numbers of fortifications, palaces and castles, monasteries and cathedrals built during their reign between 1462 and 1917, but entire towns and cultural landscapes were also created. Moscow and St Petersburg alone boast more than a hundred individual buildings listed among UNESCO's World Heritage sites.

There are thousands of fascinatingly beautiful and historically and culturally important treasures that could have been featured in this book. The book covers all the country's major regions, with particular emphasis on the regions in the west of the country, which are more easily accessible to tourists. At the same time, we have also included some relatively unknown and rarely visited destinations. Our choices were guided not least by our endeavors to paint an overall picture of the country, a picture which also mirrors some of the country's more recent and less splendid aspects. Inevitably, however, there will be much that is important to individual Russia enthusiasts that will be missing from this book but at the same time there is much new, waiting to be discovered.

I hope that your personal voyage of discovery will prove to be very enjoyable.

The Publisher

Contents

The Kremlin, Moscow

Kazan Cathedral, St Petersburg

Palace Square, St Petersburg

Solovetsky Monastery, northeastern Karelia

Sergiyev Posad Refectory, outside Moscow

Only God is above it

The **KREMLIN** is a World Heritage site, the seat of a superpower, and the heart of Moscow

LOCATION:
The Kremlin

OPENING TIMES:
Daily 10 a.m.-5 p.m., closed Thursday; entrance is through the Kutafya Tower behind the Manege

GETTING THERE:
Metro: Biblioteka Imeni Lenina, Borovitskaya, Aleksandrovskiy Sad

"Above Moscow there is only the Kremlin and above the Kremlin there is only God," goes an Old Russian saying, and as far as the Russian people are concerned, this still holds true today. At least with regard to ruling power in Russia, the Kremlin always was and still is quite simply at its center. Not only is it the seat of all political power in Russia, but it is also situated at the heart of Moscow itself. This entire complex of palaces, cathedrals and dazzling buildings sprawls over an area of 70 acres (28ha) overlooking the Moskva River, where it dominates the city's skyline.

It is here that the strands of the past and the present run together, with a magnetic attraction for power, money and, more recently, tourists.

From wooden palisades to magnificent buildings

From its earliest origins at the very heart of Moscow—in 1147—the Kremlin has grown over the course of many centuries, first from a system of simple wooden fortifications, to a fortress surrounded by a 7,330-ft (2,235-m) defense wall and finally emerging as an imposing seat of government.

Each ruler in turn has remodeled it according to his own ideas. The first was Prince Yuri Dolgorukiy "The Longhand," Moscow's founder, to whom a monument was erected in Gorky Street. In the middle of the 12th century he built a small, fortified settlement on top of the hill overlooking the Moskva. In the late 15th century, Tsar Ivan III extended the settlement by building a fortified wall incorporating 19 towers.

Since then, many generations and people from many nations have extended, rebuilt and improved the Kremlin. During the flurry of building activity that went on between 1474 and 1530, for example, Italian architects developed the site in the Milanese style. Not only did they build an elaborate defense system, consisting of imposing walls, towers, ramparts, bastions, and moats but they also built several of the Kremlin's magnificent cathedrals.

The 17th century saw the addition of slender spires to the Kremlin's towers while the Spasskaya Tower was equipped with its clock and famous carillon. At the beginning of the 18th century, Tsar Peter the Great, in his turn, produced a design for the Arsenal himself, the largest building within the Kremlin complex. The Senate Palace, the present-day seat of government, was commissioned by Catherine II ("the Great"), and in 1937, Stalin had red ruby stars installed on top of the towers. The most recent architectural addition did little to enhance the beauty of the Kremlin: in 1961, Nikita Khruschev, the then head of state, commissioned the Palace of Congresses, an unattractive modern building of glass, aluminum, concrete, and marble.

Restored to power

For all the Kremlin's impressiveness, however, Peter the Great could not resist transferring his empire's center of power to his new capital, St Petersburg. It was not until around 200 years later in the aftermath of the Revolution that Lenin restored Rus-

The Kremlin, illuminated by night in a blaze of light, is one of the city's unmistakable landmarks (below).

sia's seat of government to Moscow's Kremlin—a symbolic act representing the rebirth of the capital and its reinstatement as the center of power.

Nowadays, within the walls of the Kremlin, a museum atmosphere combines with the bustle of political life. Some parts of the Kremlin, such as the Pleasure Palace and Terem Palace, remain closed to visitors, and anyone visiting the Kremlin must be prepared to undergo rigorous security checks.

The restoration of the Kremlin, its role as the seat of government, and the representative nature of its buildings all bear testimony to the fact that the present government is at pains to preserve a sense of historical and national continuity.

The Kremlin's collection of palaces, cathedrals and towers soar above Moscow, silhouetting the city's skyline (above).

The Arsenal, with its creamy yellow façade, is the largest building complex within the walls of the Kremlin (left).

9

The world's most beautiful fortress

Not only do the **KREMLIN'S WALLS AND TOWERS** ensure the survival of the citadel but they are also extremely beautiful

LOCATION:
The Kremlin

OPENING TIMES:
Daily 10 a.m.-5 p.m., closed Thursday; entrance through the Kutafya Tower behind the Manege

GETTING THERE:
Metro: Biblioteka Imeni Lenina, Borovitskaya, Aleksandrovskiy Sad

The Kremlin is a fortress of superlatives—even down to its very walls and towers. Whether it is indeed the most beautiful fortification in the world may well be open to debate, but what is indisputable is that its 19 towers and approximately 1½ miles (2km) of red wall combine to create an ensemble so imposing and fascinating that it is perceived more as a work of art than a stronghold.

Nevertheless, the fortress was primarily intended to protect those in power—a situation which still prevails to this day. In the light of the risks now posed by terrorism, the Kremlin now effectively insulates those in government as it once did the Tsars. On important occasions, such as state visits, for example, the area is completely closed to tourists.

A long history
Tsar Ivan III commissioned the building of the Kremlin complex toward the end of the 15th century, as a symbol of his power. To this end, Italian architects of the Milanese school were summoned to Moscow, and the resulting influence of the Italian Renaissance is unmistakable.

First to be constructed, in 1485, was the Secret Tower on the southern Moskva wall, from which a secret passageway led down to the river. Two years later, the Moskva Tower was erected, also known as the Beklemishevskaya Tower, which is said to have taken its name from a boyar, whose manor lay nearby. The fact that his name was immortalized did not, however, help to save the man from a tragic fate. He was hanged a short time afterward and both his house and the tower were converted into a prison.

Mighty towers
Situated in a corner position overlooking the southern bank of the Moskva is one of the Kremlin's most beautiful towers, the strategically important Water Tower. It was later equipped with a pump, which drew water from the Moskva up into the Kremlin and ensured the citadel's water supply.

Behind it, at the most southerly point of the triangular complex is the Borovitskaya Tower, the name of which harks back to the forested hill by the same name on which the Kremlin was built.

The gateway to this mighty tower now serves as the entrance to the Kremlin. It provides access to the residence of the president. It is not only the Kremlin's dignitaries who pass through here, however; it is also the tourist entrance.

The tallest tower, the Trinity Tower, is situated on the western side. It is almost a copy of the Savior's Tower in Red Square. In front of it stands the Kutafya Tower, which, roughly translated, means "tower of bulkily clad women." The mighty Arsenal Tower occupies a corner spot along the wall adjacent to the Alexander Garden. It too concealed a spring and water supply for the Kremlin.

The Savior's Tower and St Nicholas Tower stand guard over Red Square like proud sentinels. The Savior's Tower—named for the icon mounted on it—is also renowned for its famous chimes. Long ago, these played the anthem "God Save the Tsars." Following the October Revolution, it was equipped with new chimes playing the "Internationale." Nowadays, the chimes only strike the hours. The Savior's Tower was built in 1491 by Antonio Solario—as was the nearby St Nicholas Tower. Its name stems from a mosaic of St Nicholas mounted above the gate.

The last tower to be built was the Tsar's Tower, the picturesque appearance of which is enhanced by its pyramid shapes and tent roof topped by a gilded weathervane. It was built in 1680 and was used by the Tsar's family as a viewing platform on special occasions when ceremonies were held in Red Square.

The Savior's Tower adjacent to the Manege forms the official entrance to the Kremlin. To the left and right are kiosks selling admission tickets (facing page).

In some cases, the architects of the Kremlin's towers added filigree ornamentation to their design. Some had to be rebuilt following their destruction by the French during the Napoleonic Wars (left).

The Kremlin's red wall, which is 1.2 miles (2km) in length, isolates the citadel from the rest of the town (below).

The great residences
The palaces of the Kremlin have witnessed history in the making

LOCATION:
The Kremlin

OPENING TIMES:
Daily 10 a.m.–5 p.m.,
closed Thursday;
entrance through the
Kutafya Tower, adjacent
to the Manège

GETTING THERE:
Metro: Biblioteka Imeni
Lenina, Borovitskaya,
Aleksandrovskiy Sad

The two rows of windows give the impression of a three-story building. The Palace actually has just two floors (below).

No matter how many changes Russia has gone through or how dramatically the country is changing at the present time—one thing remains incontrovertible: if one disregards the St Petersburg interlude, it is the palaces of the Kremlin that have witnessed history in the making. Three of these have been used as residences for grand dukes and Tsars, Soviet leaders and presidents: the Grand Palace, the Terem Palace, and the Faceted Palace.

Each of these buildings has undergone radical changes during the course of history and has experienced destruction, rebuilding, and restoration. They have now been restored to fresh splendor, an improvement most visitors can only appreciate from the outside, since the gates to these magnificent buildings are, as a rule, only opened to state visitors.

Vast and magnificent staterooms

The oldest of the residences on view today is the Faceted Palace, which was the first stone palace to be built within the walls of the Kremlin at the end of the 14th century. Its name is taken from its external appearance: the main façade is embellished with faceted white limestone. Inside this square building, the most impressive room is the richly decorated grand hall, an area of 5,380 square feet (500m²) in which the grand princes used to entertain their guests, celebrate victories and hold receptions.

The Terem Palace was built in 1635 during the reign of the first Tsar of the Romanov dynasty. During the 19th century, it underwent radical rebuilding work, which resulted in its present appearance. Its 11 small towers topped by gold domes are easily visible. The Terem Palace housed the private quarters of the Tsar's family, including living rooms as well as several prayer rooms. The most interesting parts of the building are undoubtedly the living quarters of the royal family, in particular the Tsarina's room, which is lavishly decorated in gold.

The Palace is furnished in a fairytale style that it is reminiscent of the Arabian Nights. It was made famous by Mussorgsky's opera *Boris Godunov* and forms the setting for key scenes portraying the downfall of Tsar Boris.

The largest and most important of the Kremlin's Palaces, the Grand Palace, was not built until the 19th century. This mighty building rises majestically along the side of the Kremlin overlooking the Moskva. The building, which was intended to replace the former Winter Palace, involved a group of several architects working to a design by Court Architect Konstantin Thon.

This Palace, with its classical and old-style Russian lines, provided a residence for those in power and is situated at the highest point of the fortifications with wonderful views over the city. With more than 700 rooms and halls, this three-winged palace complex is an extremely impressive edifice. The length of the façade alone measures 410ft (125m). The second floor has two rows of windows, one above the other, which give the impression from the outside of a three-story building.

The Grand Palace rises majestically above the tree-covered walls of the Kremlin (above).

The entrance to the Faceted Palace is by means of a large open flight of steps (left).

Superlative sights

Soaring above Cathedral Square is the city's tallest structure: **THE "IVAN THE GREAT" BELL TOWER**. At the base of the tower are the world's largest existing bell and the biggest cannon

LOCATION:
The Kremlin

OPENING TIMES:
Daily 10 a.m.–5 p.m., entrance through Kutafya Tower, adjacent to the Manege

GETTING THERE:
Metro: Biblioteka Imeni Lenina, Borovitskaya Aleksandrovskiy Sad

A Tsar who never uttered a sound: nick-named "Tsar Kolokol," this bell, the largest in the world, never chimed, as it fell to the ground in a fire before it was ever sounded (right).

Likewise, the world's biggest cannon, which stands at the base of the Bell Tower, was never fired (below).

The Kremlin was for a long time not only Russia's power center, but also the spiritual heart of the country. This is particularly evident in the impressive cathedrals and religious buildings within the fortress walls.

These were built not least because the secular leaders of the 15th century believed that one important way of demonstrating their power was to build imposing religious buildings. Following the fall of the Byzantine Empire in 1453, Tsar Ivan III revealed his imperial designs and also demanded leadership of the Ortho-dox Church. He declared himself the head of Orthodox Christianity and aspired to make Moscow the succes-sor to Rome and Constantinople. He dreamed of creating a "Third Rome"—the distinctive landmarks of which would be the incomparable churches of the Kremlin.

Building the Bell Tower
In order to do this, Ivan III's first step was to demolish the old churches in Moscow. He then commissioned the building of an impressive bell tower which, owing to its architectural style, was also known as the "Burning Can-dle." Its towering height and sonorous chimes were intended to signal Moscow's allegiance to the "proper" faith. Architect Bon Friazin's design was built on an octagonal site and comprised three stories, each with open arcades for bells. On the ground floor is the largely unvisited John Kli-makos Church.

Later completion
The building was eventually complet-ed in 1600 by Tsar Boris Godunov, who succeeded Tsar Ivan IV, in place of the latter's unstable son Fyodor. Boris Godunov was immortalized not only thanks to the "Ivan the Great" Bell Tower (in Russian: *Ivan Velikiy*), but also as a result of Pushkin's drama and Mussorgsky's opera of the same name.

He added the following inscription in the bell tower under the Golden Cupola: "By the grace of the Holy Trin-ity and by order of the Tsar and Grand Prince of all Russia, Boris Fedorovich, and his son, the honourable Tsarevich and Grand Prince of all Russia, Fyo-dor Borisovich, this temple was fin-ished and gilded in the summer of their reign [or 1600, according to the Western calendar]." It was subse-quently forbidden to erect any build-ing in Moscow that was higher than the tower—at least during the time of the Tsars.

With a total height of 265ft (81m), the Bell Tower was, for a long time, Moscow's tallest building. From here there are wonderful views over the city, which have, in the past, been enjoyed by many visitors. Unfortunately, since the October Revolution of 1917, tourists have not been permitted to climb the tower.

The heaviest bell

The Bell Tower, situated at the political and religious heart of Moscow, was equipped with the world's heaviest bell, the "Queen of Bells," also known as "Tsar Kolokol." In the end,

it never actually rang out to call the faithful to the cathedrals as the tower burned down before the first chimes could sound. Tsar Kolokol fell into the moat around the Kremlin and a section weighing 12.6 tons (11.5 metric tonnes) broke off. The bell remained on the ground for almost a hundred years before the entire 220 ton (200 metric tonne) giant was raised and displayed on a granite base.

The Tsar's Cannon

Situated next to the world's biggest bell is the world's largest cannon: "Tsar Pushka," or the "Tsar's Can-

non." In the same way as the bell never chimed, the cannon, which was cast in 1586, never actually fired a shot. With a calibre of 890mm, a length of 17.5ft (5.34m) and weighing 44 tons (40 metric tonnes), it is not so much a testimony to Tsarist military might, but more of a showpiece in the art of casting guns. The barrel of the cannon is decorated with a relief depicting Tsar Fyodor Ivanovich.

The "Ivan the Great" Bell Tower remained Moscow's tallest building for hundreds of years. Situated in front of it are the world's largest bell and the world's biggest cannon.

The Kremlin's crowning glories

The Cathedral of the Deposition of the Robe and the Cathedral of the Annunciation were the private churches used by the country's rulers

LOCATION:
The Kremlin

OPENING TIMES:
Daily 10 a.m.–5 p.m.,
closed Thursdays;
entrance through
Kutafya Tower, adjacent
to the Manège

GETTING THERE:
Metro: Biblioteka Imeni
Lenina, Borovitskaya,
Aleksandrovskiy Sad

It is not the Kremlin's secular buildings that dominate the town—it is the gold and silver domes of the churches which, quite literally, present the dazzling high points. There are altogether six cathedrals and several other churches, all grouped around a small square known as Cathedral Square. They include the private churches of Russia's secular rulers and religious authorities: the Cathedral of the Annunciation that belonged to the Tsars and the Cathedral of the Deposition of the Robe, which served as a domestic chapel to Patriarchs of the church. The history of both these churches began in 1485 when, as part of a major rebuilding project in the Kremlin, they were built on the foundations of older structures.

The "gold-topped" cathedral

This rather fanciful and most picturesque building was designed by the best architects in Pskov. Following a fire in the mid-16th century, Ivan the Terrible not only had the church restored, but took the opportunity to enlarge it. Since this time, the Cathedral of the Annunciation has been nicknamed the "gold-topped" thanks to the addition not only of four further chapels, but also a total of nine golden cupolas, which gleam in the sunlight—commemorating the nine-day battle against the Tatars in Kazan.

The galleries, decorated with scenes from the Old Testament, lead into the interior of the cathedral. A pair of pillars with Corinthian capitals and decorated in the classical style with upward-pointing acanthus leaves, frame the sky-blue portals, the ornamentation of which reflects stylistic elements of the early Italian Renaissance. The cathedral's royal atmosphere is reinforced by the floor, paved with magnificent agate and red jasper.

This royal court was particularly favored by the Tsars and grand princes for weddings and family baptisms, occasions which obviously demanded a splendid setting, and to this end the Tsars decorated their private cathedral with a particularly special treasure: the first and also one of the finest iconostases in all Russia.

The iconostasis combines the work of two of the greatest Russian icon painters, the monk, Andrei Rublyev and Theophanes the Greek, who created a wooden wall with three doors, decorated with icons, all featuring a specific set of images, which separated the altar room from the main area.

These artists belong to the great Moscow school of icon painters whose work is renowned for their use

Just one cupola crowns the simple Cathedral of the Deposition of the Robe, tucked away in the shadow of the mighty Cathedral of the Assumption and the Kremlin Palace, shown here with the 11 golden cupolas of the Terem Palace (right).

A small museum is attached to the Patriarch's church, in which valuable friezes are on display, depicting, for example, the Crucifixion of Christ (below).

The domes of the Cathedral of the Annunciation, which served as the venue for the Tsars' family ceremonies, can be seen above the Kremlin (right).

of luminescent colors and transparent light as well as their fine brushwork. The names of Andrei Rublyev and Theophanes the Greek are as famous in Russia today as are those of well-known Western painters in Europe.

Simple beauty

In contrast to all the splendors of the Tsars' church, the Patriarchs' cathedral, with its surprising simplicity and well-defined proportions, is more reflective of the traditional and purist style of the Orthodox Church. The Deposition of the Robe Cathedral is a classical-style four-column church in the shape of a cross and topped by a single dome. Nevertheless, the building, with its pastel-colored frescoes, has a unique beauty that inspired the church leaders of the day to deep devotion and quiet prayer.

A small museum is now attached to the cathedral, in which are displayed exhibits dating from its days as the residence of the Patriarchs.

The Tsars' resting place

The Archangel Cathedral houses the tombs of the Tsars

LOCATION:
The Kremlin

OPENING TIMES:
Daily 10 a.m.–5 p.m.,
closed Thursday;
entrance through
Kutafya Tower, adjacent
to the Manege

GETTING THERE:
Metro: Biblioteka Imeni
Lenina, Borovitskaya,
Aleksandrovskiy Sad

The interior of the cathedral is decorated primarily with portraits of the Grand Princes who are buried here and with frescoes depicting the Archangel Michael with an upraised sword in his hand (below).

Tsar Ivan Kalita, who ruled Russia at the end of the 15th and the beginning of the 16th century, wanted to create a fitting burial place for himself and his successors. For a true Tsar such as himself, only a new cathedral would suffice and in 1505, an Italian, Alovisio Nuovo, was commissioned to design the building. So it was that the Archangel Cathedral was erected on the site of an older church dating from the 14th century and dedicated to Michael the Archangel, the protector of Moscow's rulers. The youngest of the Kremlin's magnificent churches in Cathedral Square, this church stands out in a variety of ways.

In just three years, the Venetian-born architect built a palace-style church in the traditional Russian cross-shaped, domed style. It consists of a central cupola and four smaller domes—the only ones to shimmer in silver among the group of Kremlin churches.

An architectural style that became a school

Another unique aspect of the Archangel Cathedral is the fact that the façade is decorated with classical motifs borrowed from the Italian Renaissance. Flowers, mythical animals, arabesques and candelabras—popular themes of classical architecture—decorate the white limestone portals. The exterior design of the cathedral, completed in 1508, created

a new trend during the decades that followed as the façades of many more churches throughout Russia were decorated in a similar fashion.

In contrast to its splendid and inviting external appearance, the interior of the cathedral is very simple and rather cheerless. The vaulting, despite its formidable height, creates a rather oppressive atmosphere. The supporting columns stand very close together and all the walls inside the church are painted with frescoes. This gives the interior a gloomy atmosphere, which is more evocative of the numerous funerals held within its walls than of joyous services.

Several of the cathedral's icons on the north and south walls are dedicated to Archangel Michael and his deeds. He is said to have guided the deceased into the world beyond when their souls left their bodies. He was also revered as the leader of the heavenly hordes and has been immortal-

ized here in frescoes depicting him fighting the Tatars with an upraised sword in his hand.

Most of the wall paintings, however, are portraits of the people buried here. Depictions of 60 rulers can be seen beneath their name saints. Ivan Kalita was the first to be ceremoniously entombed here after his death in 1341. He was followed by all the other grand princes until Fyodor Alexeyevich—the brother of Peter the Great who was the last to be laid to rest in the church in a royal sarcophagus in 1682. The most interesting among this collection of tombs, representing over 300 years of history, are those of the Tsarevich Dmitriy and Ivan the Terrible. After Peter the Great moved to Petersburg in 1712, all subsequent Tsars were laid to rest in the Peter and Paul Cathedral in that city.

The Cathedral of the Archangel Michael, the last resting place of the Tsars, is the youngest of all the Kremlin's churches (above).

The silver cupolas of the Archangel Cathedral make a delightful contrast to the large golden cupola.

The Coronation Cathedral

The Kremlin's largest and most magnificent church was once at the heart of the country's religious life

LOCATION:
The Kremlin

OPENING TIMES:
Daily 10 a.m.-5 p.m.,
closed Thursdays;
entrance through
Kutafya Tower, adjacent
to the Manege

GETTING THERE:
Metro: Biblioteka Imeni
Lenina, Borovitskaya,
Aleksandrovskiy Sad

No other church within the Kremlin walls was as important as the Cathedral of the Assumption. It was here that the Tsars were crowned, the Metropolitans inaugurated and Russian generals blessed before going to war. It was once at the heart of the Russian Orthodox faith and for a long time the religious center of Russia. It also housed one of the greatest treasures of the Orthodox Church: the miracle-performing icon of Our Lady of Vladimir, now on display in the Tretyakov Gallery.

The cathedral's unusual name is derived from the Feast of the Dormition, "the falling-asleep of Our Holy Lady, the Mother of God and Perpetual Virgin Mary," which equates with the Roman Catholic Feast of the Assumption of Mary. For this reason, it is also known as the Cathedral of the Assumption.

This imposing building, for which Ivan III laid the foundation stone at the end of the 15th century on the site of Moscow's first stone church, was conceived from the beginning as a place where coronation ceremonies would be held. The Tsar commissioned Italian architect Aristotele Fiovaranti, who designed a particularly splendid church modeled on the similarly-named Cathedral of Vladimir. And with very good reason since up until then Vladimir had been the religious center of Russian princedom. Now, however, Metropolitan Pyotr

Amazing chandeliers illuminate the interior of the cathedral, in which Tsars were once crowned, Metropolitans inaugurated, and military generals blessed before battle (facing page).

The Tsars used to enter the cathedral through the richly decorated southern portal, which combines old-style Russian architecture with the influence of the Italian Renaissance (left).

More than a hundred icon painters were involved in the third session of painting. Old frescoes were copied and renewed (below).

was to take up his ruling seat in the Kremlin and Moscow was to become the new home of the Metropolitans. The church's design was intended to reflect the traditional Russian style, thereby expressing respect for the church's history, while the influence of the Italian Renaissance was a way of signaling a new era.

The interior of the richly painted and beautifully decorated Cathedral reveals itself to the visitor as a vast hall, divided by rhythmically arranged pillars. Particularly worthy of note—together with the precious iconostasis—is Ivan IV's prayer stool with its unique wood-carvings. There are also numerous interesting icons, including those of St George, which originate from as early as the 12th century.

Seat of the religious rulers

The Patriarch's Palace, adjoining the Cathedral of the Twelve Apostles, is the residence of the head of the Russian-Orthodox Christian church

LOCATION:
The Kremlin

OPENING TIMES:
Daily 10 a.m.-5 p.m., closed Thursday; entrance through the Kutafya Tower, adjacent to the Manege

GETTING THERE:
Metro: Biblioteka Imeni Lenina, Borovitskaya, Aleksandrovskiy Sad

The precious iconostasis in the Cathedral of the Twelve Apostles originates from the Ascension Monastery, which Stalin had demolished (above).

Though never wielding quite as much power as the Tsars, the Patriarchs, who were the religious leaders of the Orthodox Church, nevertheless exercised a strong influence. Throughout the centuries, there were many occasions when they played a key role in influencing Russian history. It is hardly surprising, therefore, that the Tsars were constantly that at pains to retain their allegiance and conversely, the Patriarchs strove to maintain their considerable influence over the secular rulers.

After the fall of the Byzantine Empire, the Russian bishops, who had until then been subordinate to the Patriarch of Constantinople, decided to break away from the mother church. They moved to Moscow, where the Metropolitans occupied a palace to the north of the Cathedral of the Assumption, which became the seat of the Patriarch.

The 17th century saw a period of particularly intensive cooperation between the secular and religious powers in Russia: at the beginning of this century Metropolitan Filaret, who was also father of Tsar Michael, held the strings of Russian politics firmly in his hand.

In 1652, Nikon took over the office of Patriarch. From the start, he too made sure of his influence over the young Alexander I, who had just ascended to the Tsarist throne. He was constantly on hand to dispense fatherly advice on all-important matters.

Symbols of power

As a clear demonstration of the extent of his power, Nikon had the old wooden palace in the Kremlin demolished and in its place a splendid new residence was constructed. The Patriarch's Palace with the adjoining Cathedral of the Twelve Apostles which, viewed from the main entrance to the Kremlin, are in front of Cathedral Square.

Nikon was an aggressive man who pushed through a large number of liturgical reforms, encountering as a result a great deal of bitter opposition. This led to a temporary schism in the Orthodox Church and signaled the beginning of the end of Nikon's rule. His increased striving to gain more and more secular power helped contribute to his fall from grace with the Tsar, who had meanwhile become more assertive. Eventually, in 1666 the Moscow Synod relieved Nikon of his

office and stripped him of his title. Despite this, the reforms he had instituted remained in force.

The Synod met in the so-called Cross Chamber, a magnificent room, measuring 2,690ft² (250m²), in the Patriarch's Palace, which Nikon had commissioned. This great hall, which is covered with an unsupported vault, is well worth a visit. Not only did the bishops meet here, but it was also used for state banquets. The Cross Chamber and adjoining rooms of the Patriarch's Palace are now open to visitors and include a museum with a display charting Russian ecclesiastical history.

The Palace melts seamlessly into the Cathedral of the Twelve Apostles. Its ground-plan and design are both based on old-style Russian churches. In this way, Nikon was deliberately trying to indicate that, despite his reforms, he nevertheless upheld the traditions of the Orthodox faith. The church, topped by five cupolas, is the smallest of the Kremlin's cathedrals. One of its main treasures is an iconostasis, which originally came from the Ascension Monastery, which subsequently destroyed following the October Revolution.

The Cathedral of the Twelve Apostles and adjoining Patriarch's Palace are based upon old-style Russian architecture (above).

The Patriach's Palace houses a small museum containing a display of items charting Russian ecclesiastical history, including this valuable writing desk which once belonged to the Patriarch.

Treasures of the Tsars

The Armory houses the legendary gold of the Tsars

LOCATION:
The Kremlin

OPENING TIMES:
Daily 10 a.m.–5 p.m., closed Thursday; entrance through the Kutafya Tower, adjacent to the Manege

GETTING THERE:
Metro: Biblioteka Imeni Lenina, Borovitskaya, Aleksandrovskiy Sad

The Armory houses one of the world's largest treasure troves, featuring some indescribably precious exhibits. These include not only the crown jewels, but also items of furniture, such as this gold table (below).

Sable-trimmed crowns and ceremonial insignia studded with precious stones: diamond jewelry and superb Fabergé eggs; plates fashioned from solid gold and ruby-studded goblets; sumptuous vestments belonging to Catherine and Peter made from the finest, most costly embroidered fabrics; magnificent carriages and ceremonial harnesses decorated with precious gems; beautifully crafted arms and elaborately forged weaponry; incomparable icons and priceless handwritten documents. The Armory, the Tsars' Museum in Moscow's Kremlin, houses treasures of inestimable value. It can justifiably claim to be one of the greatest treasure chambers in the world, if not the greatest of all.

Almost all the items on display were once privately owned by the Tsars. Looking at them, it almost seems as if the Russian rulers were constantly vying with one another in opulence and jewelry: Ivan IV, for example, sat on an ivory throne; Boris Godunov occupied a throne finished in gold leaf and studded with 2,000 precious stones; and Mikhail Fyodorovich held court from a diamond throne from Persia (now Iran). A visit to this treasure chamber represents a journey into the history of Russia and the Tsars.

Ivan's "blood gold"

The story of this treasure, which is steeped in legend, begins with Ivan the Terrible, who was obsessed by an insatiable greed for gold and sable, which at that time was as valuable as gold. It was this greed which earned the Tsar the title "Terrible." He, like no other ruler before or after him, systematically plundered the country, totally obsessed with the idea of filling his treasury and it was he who first built a chamber within the Kremlin to hoard his "blood gold."

The Tsars not only accumulated their treasures as spoils from their conquests and subsequent pillaging, they also employed armorers and craftsmen, whose workshops, which flourished in particular during the middle of the 17th century, were situated in the Armory.

The building that stands today was built in the mid-19th century and functioned both as the Treasury and the Tsar's workshop. The complex was largely dedicated to the manufacture of weapons—it once housed the country's biggest armory, from which it derives its rather bland-sounding name.

In 1851, Nicholas I commissioned the court architect Konstantin Thon to design the building in the Russian style. As well as functioning as a new production center, he also intended it to function as Russia's first museum for the collection of what were already world famous treasures.

Exhibition of profligacy

Following the October Revolution, one of Lenin's first decrees was designed to protect the treasures of the Armory from any plundering. A short time later, the chamber of treasures was opened up to the public. The Soviets' motive in doing so was aimed not at allowing people to admire these treasures of cultural history, but at demonstrating to the proletariat the profligacy of the Tsars.

The most precious items are displayed in the so-called Diamond Fund exhibition where visitors can admire the heavily guarded Crown jewels, protected behind bullet-proof glass. One of the most significant treasures is the Crown of Catherine II, which is studded with 5,000 diamonds.

The Armory, the Tsars' museum in the Kremlin, is contained in a complex of buildings designed in the Russian style by Konstantin Thon in 1851 (left).

On view behind the glass cabinets is a collection of the Tsars' elaborately decorated silver and gold tableware–symbols not only of their great wealth, but also of their extravagance (below).

Historic Alexander Garden

Situated between the Kremlin and the Manege is a green oasis in the midst of the hectic bustle of the city

Russia ○Moscow

LOCATION:
Manezhnaya Uliza; along the western Kremlin wall

GETTING THERE:
Metro: Biblioteka Imeni Lenina, Aleksandrovskiy Sad

The Alexander Garden surrounds the Kremlin like a green belt (above).

Memorial to the Unknown Soldier (facing page, above right).

Mounted police uphold law and order (right).

In winter, the slopes are a favorite place for children with sleds (far right).

26

Between the gates of the Kremlin and the Manege is a small green area—Alexander Garden. The term "garden" is perhaps a bit misleading in this case, however, since Alexander Garden is a combination of park, memorial garden, cemetery and sculptural display.

Its origins reach back to Ivan IV, who had various herbs and remedial plants grown here for use in the royal apothecary, which was situated nearby on the site of what is now the Russian Museum.

The beginning of the 19th century saw Alexander I on the throne of Russia. The Tsar conceived a desire for a stretch of green parkland where he could stroll, and accordingly commissioned the architect Osip Bove to redesign the area. To gain more space, the latter began by diverting the small Neglinnaya River, which used to flow around the Kremlin, through an underground aqueduct. Bove not only created areas of greenery but also created an ornate ruined "grotto" along the wall of the Kremlin, a secluded spot much favored as a meeting-place for lovers.

Promenade and memorial avenue

The Alexander Garden, named after the Tsar who commissioned it, soon became a popular hub of court and social life. After the October Revolution, the Soviets converted it into a

place of commemoration, installing a Memorial to the Unknown Soldier in the upper part of the garden.

The tomb was erected to mark the 25th anniversary of the victory against the Germans. It was erected above the remains of soldiers who fell during World War II and bears the inscription: "Your name is unknown, your deed is immortal."

In front of the memorial burns the "Eternal Flame of Glory" with two soldiers providing a guard of honor. The guard is changed every hour, a spectacle that is particularly popular with tourists.

Alongside the memorial are the commemorative blocks of red porphyry filled with soil from the "hero cities" of Leningrad (now renamed St Petersburg), Kiev, Minsk, Volgograd, Sevastopol, Odessa, Kerch, Novorossiysk, Tula and Brest, cities which all endured heavy fighting during World War II.

Green sanctuary

This narrow strip of green, which runs from the Historical Museum to the Arsenal Tower, forms a small verdant oasis in the midst of what is now a noisy and hectic city center. As in the days of Alexander I, it is still a pleasant place to rest in the shadow of the Kremlin Wall. During the summer children splash about in the fountains and in winter the gentle slopes alongside the Kremlin are a favorite place for sledding.

The Manege

The army's parade hall mirrors the history of the city

LOCATION:
Manezhnaya Ploshad; on the northwestern side of the Kremlin

GETTING THERE:
Metro: Ploshad Revolutsii, Okhotny Ryad

A large gilt fountain forms the impressive heart of the underground shopping center (right).

Equestrian statues (below) in front of the long row of pillars are a reminder of the original purpose of the Manege as a parade arena and exercise hall.

Stretching out behind the Kremlin, Alexander Garden, and the Russian Museum is the vast Manege Square—the bustling and popular center of Moscow life. It is here that people meet to shop in the huge subterranean shopping center, to begin their stroll along the Tverskaya shopping mile or to visit one of the city's largest group of cultural buildings: the Manege.

This eye-catching and imposing group of buildings owes its existence to the most significant event in Moscow's architectural history: in 1812, the citizens of Moscow set fire to their own city to leave Napoleon facing an inglorious, supposed victory. The fire destroyed three quarters of the buildings and Napoleon entered Moscow to find it in ashes. This marked the beginning of the end of his Russian campaign.

When Napoleon and his army were forced to retreat from Russia, defeated by hunger and fatigue, Tsar Alexander I commissioned a major building project to commemorate the victory over the Grande Armée: a parade hall for the Officers' School. The result was the Manege, in which a company of 2,000 men could perform riding exhibitions.

Alexander I commissioned Agustin de Betancourt y Molina, a Spanish engineer who became a Russian general, to construct a clearly struc-

tured building, the planned function of which called for remarkable dimensions. It was to measure 557ft by 147ft (170m x 45 m) and would be topped by an enormous roof construction, uniquely without internal support. The simplicity, massiveness and austerity of this unique structure are, even today, a source of fascination. Between 1823 and 1835, the building was redesigned in the classical style of Osip Bove.

From 1831 the Manege was used for exhibitions and fairs—thus setting the scene for its later use as a cultural center. Today it is mainly used as a complex for exhibitions and art fairs.

The Manege was destroyed by fire in March 2004. It is almost certain that the fire was started deliberately to make way for the construction of lucrative new housing on the site. The ill-conceived plan came to nought, however, thanks to efforts on the part of the conservation authorities and fortunately this cultural monument was rebuilt—a restoration which was not necessarily a foregone conclusion in a city where cultural monuments still tend to simply disappear.

Despite numerous fires, the Manege has always risen from its ashes–most recently in 2004 when it is believed arsonists attempted to destroy the building.

The glass dome of the subterranean shopping mall, which resembles the earth's sphere, is situated in the center of the landscaped square in front of the Manege (below).

The city center

Red Square is the most beautiful of the city's squares

LOCATION:
Krasnaya Ploshad; on the northeastern side of the Kremlin

GETTING THERE:
Metro: Ploshad Revolyutsii

Lenin's final resting-place in Red Square was also used for another purpose: the Soviet leaders viewed their parades from the balustrades of the mausoleum (below).

Krasnaya ploshad—translated, it means "beautiful square" and as anyone who has been to Russia's most famous square will know, it justifiably deserves the name. Bordered by the walls of the Kremlin, St. Basil's Cathedral, the GUM department store, and the Historical Museum, the square is, architecturally speaking, the most spectacular the city has to offer.

The fact that it is now known as "Red Square" is due largely to the Soviet leadership which, in the aftermath of the October Revolution, took advantage of the fact that the word *krasnyi* can mean both "beautiful" as well as "red."

Once a market square and later a center for elegant shops, Moscow's most famous square was used each year by the Soviets as an arena for military parades. Such military march-pasts featuring weaponry and troops have, however, long been a thing of the past. The paved square with its symbolic monuments is now primarily the domain of the public who enjoy a stroll through the city center.

Place of history

Covering an area of almost 807,000ft^2 (75,000m^2), Red Square is not very vast, yet no other arena in Russian history has ever played a more important role. It was here that the Tsar's soldiers paid homage to their sovereign and here too that decrees were proclaimed and the heads of rebels rolled. The Church used the square for its ceremonial processions and people celebrated their festivals here.

The Soviets likewise chose this traditional square for their own celebrations: when World War II ended, the flags of the defeated German Wehrmacht were brought here and torched; and Yuri Gagarin, the first man in space, greeted his jubilant fellow countrymen in this historic square in 1961.

Lenin's final resting-place

The potentates of the Communist era were laid to rest along the Kremlin Wall. The most famous of these was Vladimir Ilyich Ulanyov, better known as Lenin, who lies in a glass sarcophagus within a mausoleum, which is built of dark red porphyry and black labradorite. A special institute exists, which has, for many decades, had the responsibility of looking after the embalmed body.

The days when long queues would form outside Lenin's mausoleum are long since past, however, and nowadays, this is a quiet spot with a much more relaxed and tranquil atmosphere, which was designated as a World Cultural Heritage Site in 1990.

Two sides of one of the world's most famous squares: on the city side, the Historical Museum protects Red Square from the traffic and bustle of the big city (left).

The more familiar view looks toward St Basil's Cathedral, the most beautiful building on this historic site (below).

Beginning in 1990, St. Basil's Cathedral was fully restored over the course of 16 years and since 2006 has stood in its newly acquired splendor. The cupolas, in particular, look as if they have only just been erected.

Symbols of Moscow

No other building in Moscow is as famous the world over as the fairy-tale St Basil's Cathedral in Red Square

Moscow
Russia

LOCATION:
Krasnaya Ploshad 4, on the southern side of Red Square

OPENING TIMES:
Daily 11 a.m.-4 p.m., closed Tuesday

GETTING THERE:
Metro: Ploshad Revolyutsii, Okhotny Ryad

It graces the front of virtually every book on Moscow, it is photographed thousands of times a day and it can be seen on most picture postcards: the colorful, fascinatingly beautiful St Basil's Cathedral in Red Square. It is not the Kremlin, but this church which is the real symbol of Moscow—and, by extension, of all Russia. No other Russian building is as famous throughout the world as this cathedral.

Ivan the Terrible commissioned this massive building after his historic victory over the Tatars. The cathedral therefore constitutes a reminder of one of the most important turning points in Russian history: the invasion of Kazan on October 1st 1552. This marked the end of centuries of domination by the Tatars, thereby laying the foundation for the future multinationalist Russian state.

It was the Tsar's wish that the cathedral's size and design should reflect this triumphal victory. Two architects, Postnik and Barma, were commissioned with the building of this church, which, with its colorful domes, is so un-Russian in appearance. Some mystery remains, however, as to whether there was in fact just one architect by the name of Postnik Barma Yakovlev.

The cathedral consists of eight chapels, which encircle a ninth, the central spired church. This is the original Church of the Intercession of the Virgin, which gave its name to the cathedral. Looking up into its tower reveals the height of the structure (right).

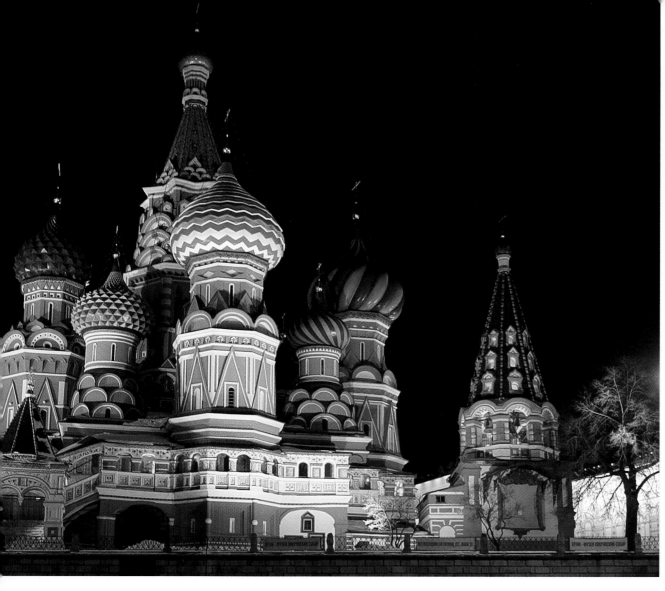

Night or day, St Basil's Cathedral is the most photographed building in the city. The church, around which many legends have been woven, was commissioned by Ivan the Terrible to commemorate the historic victory over the Tatars.

Myths and legends

The story has it that the cruel Tsar Ivan had his architect blinded after the cathedral was completed so that he would never again be able to create anything that could rival its beauty.

This could well be another myth, however, for the same architect is also said to have added a small chapel a few years later—a building which gave the cathedral the name by which it is known today, St Basil's Chapel. The church was originally called the Cathedral of the Intercession of the Virgin on the Moat because the conquest of Kazan coincided with the feast day of the Intercession of the Virgin.

The name "Basil" derives from a holy man, who was laid to rest in the above-mentioned chapel. His name was Vasiliy Blazhenny, "Basil the Blessed." He is said to have lived in the Kremlin as a court fool, a reputation that enabled him to confront the Tsars about irregularities without fear of punishment. The citizens of Moscow held him so much in awe on this account that no sooner was the chapel completed than it became known as "St Basil's Cathedral."

Fixed ground-plan pattern

At first glance, it seems as if the building's architects had constructed the building in a haphazard fashion, but actually quite the opposite is true: the areas of the church are arranged in a strict geometrical pattern.

The basic plan follows a uniform cross. At each corner and in the cen-
ter is a chapel. These outer chapels were linked together by connecting rooms, each of which was similarly equipped with an altar. These were likewise topped with a dome. The result is a circle of eight chapels, in the center of which is the main body of the church.

A closer inspection of the cathedral reveals its basic structure more clearly—the central part of the church is topped by a tall, pointed tower, crowned by a golden cupola. The four chapels at the outer points of the arms of the cross are larger than the smaller domes above the connecting rooms. The reason why the design of the structure is somewhat difficult to grasp is partly because the domes are decorated in a variety of colors and partly because each façade is rendered in a different finish.

Symbolic architecture

The design of St Basil's Cathedral has a special significance. Whether this was intended from the beginning or whether the building was imbued with this interpretation at a later date is a moot point. Either way, the nine chapels are said to have been so designed because the siege of Kazan lasted eight days—hence the eight outer chapels—and the main church symbolizes the ninth day, on which the Tatar capital fell into the Tsar's hands.

Alternatively, the significance can be explained by the fact that the eight outer chapels represent the sum of three—representing the Trinity—
plus five—the triumphal number of the Pantocrator (Christ as ruler of the world).

Small interior rooms

In contrast to its extravagant, lavish and fairytale-like exterior, the interior of the cathedral is much less spectacular. There is no mighty nave to greet the visitor, just a series of corridors and small chapels. It is a long while since any services were held here—St Basil's Cathedral has been a museum since the October Revolution—but Moscow's most famous church is well worth a visit, not least in order to marvel at the wonderful views over the Kremlin and Red Square.

The interior of the Cathedral is divided into eight small chapels, which now serve as a museum.

A palace for shoppers

The GUM building, housing Russia's largest department store and constituting one of the most beautiful temples to consumerism, completes the spectacular collection of buildings in Red Square

LOCATION:
Krasnaya Ploshad 3, on the eastern side of Red Square

OPENING TIMES:
Daily 10 a.m.–10 p.m.

GETTING THERE:
Metro: Ploshad Revolyutsii, Okhotny Ryad, Kitay-Gorod

There are few department stores in the world which enjoy an international reputation, but the "State Department Store," the *Gosudarstvennyi Universal'nyi Magazin*, or GUM for short, is certainly one of these. This is not just because of its spectacular position in Red Square: GUM is, architecturally speaking, an extremely impressive center of commerce with a unique as well as exclusive range of shops.

The very dimensions of the building, which resembles a small town with its miniature passageways, bridges and galleries, are extremely impressive in themselves: measuring 820ft (250m) in length and covering an area of over 807,000ft^2 (75,000m^2), it houses 150 individual shops offering an almost fairytale shopping experience whereby no wish need remain unfulfilled.

This was not always the case, however. Under the planned economy of the Soviet government, the needs of the capital's inhabitants were calculated in advance. The allocation per capita was usually very limited. Even so, the GUM department store was always a much-coveted temple of consumerism to all Soviet citizens, and the choice of goods was naturally much greater than in the far-flung corners of this giant empire. It often happened that visitors to Moscow from other parts of the country bought up the goods from under the very noses of the Muscovites.

Commercial center with tradition

The GUM store grew from a number of individual stores that once traded here. In 1888, Nicholas II commissioned St Petersburg architect Pomer-anzev to oversee the rebuilding, a project which took until 1894. The result was a magnificent building that not only caters for every commercial need, but at the same time brings beauty and splendor to Moscow's architectural center.

The three avenues of shops on two levels, which run alongside each other, are linked by a delicate glass roof, an architectural device that lends this great building a certain air of lightness.

Nowadays, there are more millionaires in Moscow than anywhere else in the world. When they go shopping, the GUM is their first choice: it contains outlets for all the top fashion names. All the top quality items and very expensive goods are available here: from luxury watches to designer fashion.

Not only is GUM one of the largest but it is also one of the most beautiful department stores in the world (above).

The richly ornamented façade is illuminated at Christmas with thousands of lights (lower left).

Three glass-covered passageways contain outlets for the top luxury brands and many elegant boutiques (lower right).

Testament to a living faith

The Church to the Virgin of Kazan is a place of contemplation and prayer in Red Square

LOCATION:
Nikolskaya ul. 3

OPENING TIMES:
Daily 8 a.m.-7 p.m.

GETTING THERE:
Metro: Okhotny Ryad

The Church to the Virgin of Kazan is a small and rather squat edifice situated between the magnificent Historical Museum and the GUM building. Its cheerful red and white façade exudes an air of self-assurance and sets it somewhat apart from its otherwise monumental surroundings—as was deliberately intended. On the periphery of this otherwise busy square, it represents a place of tranquillity and faith—and precisely because of this, it is a magnet for visitors.

Kazan Cathedral, as the church is known, is a symbol of living faith in Russia. The striving for Western standards, for a modern lifestyle with luxury and status symbols is omnipresent in Moscow. The depth of the Orthodox faith among its people, however, is equally indisputable.

Even the severe repressive measures on the part of the Soviets could do nothing to shake it. Not only did the Communists—like Napoleon—misuse churches and monasteries as stables and prisons, but Christians throughout the country were actively persecuted and interned in camps. By the mid-1930s, only a handful of churches remained in which the liturgy could still be read. Wherever possible, churches and monasteries were demolished.

All this changed dramatically after the downfall of the Soviets. Nowadays, the Russian Orthodox Church is enjoying a veritable renaissance. Not only have possessions confiscated by the State been returned to the Church, but churches and monasteries all over the country have been renovated. In 2006, President Putin, who actively proclaimed his faith, ordered the reintroduction of religious education in state schools.

Kazan Cathedral represents a particularly eloquent monument to the recent history of the Orthodox

Above the entrance is a large mosaic depicting the icon to the Virgin of Kazan (above, right).

This diminutive church set amidst the large buildings in Red Square has a cheerful and self-assured air (facing page).

The holy icon can once again be revered in its own church (below).

Church in Russia—and not just because of its prominent position.

A church to house an icon

In 1612, Prince Pozharsky liberated Moscow and Russia from its Polish-Lithuanian aggressors. He carried with him an icon of the Virgin of Kazan. From this time onward, the icon has been attributed with divine powers and revered accordingly. In 1635, a church was specially constructed to house it in Red Square. This was designed in typical Russian style.

Stalin, however, saw it merely as a hindrance to his May Day and Revolutionary parades and had it torn down. The holy icon went missing for a while until this most holy of Russian relics was discovered to have found a safe refuge in the Vatican.

The advent of Perestroika in 1990 brought with it the revival of the

Church, a turn of events which had long been regarded as inconceivable. It was rebuilt in its original form on its old site and in 2004, Pope John Paul II returned the icon of the Virgin of Kazan, which he himself greatly revered, to the Russian Orthodox Church. In doing so, he was signaling a reconciliation between the Churches of East and West.

Once again, the faithful can pay homage to their holy relic. The guarded door of Kazan Cathedral is open every day to anyone seeking intercession or solace in the midst of the bustle of the metropolis. It is not only old Russian women, who seek it out—many young people are also followers of the faith, demonstrating that the Orthodox religion continues to thrive.

Great history

The State Historical Museum charts Russia's development from its earliest beginnings to the present day

LOCATION:
Kranaya pl. 1 / 2

OPENING TIMES:
Daily, except Tuesday, 11 a.m-7 p.m., closed first Monday in the month

GETTING THERE:
Metro: Ploshad Revolyutsii.

The rich ornamentation of the exterior of the Historical Museum is echoed by the lavish décor inside the building. Of special note are the ceiling paintings in the main entrance hall which depict well-known Russian figures (below).

On the other side of Red Square is the State Historical Museum, the mighty architectural counterpart to the romantic structure of St Basil's Cathedral. This imposing red brick building separates this famous square from the bustling city. Its ornate main façade, characterized by numerous small turrets, decorative cornices and tent-top roofs, has the appearance of a fairytale castle, which has inadvertently strayed into the big city.

This impression was in fact created deliberately: in 1872, when the Archeological Society commissioned the building of a new Museum in Red Square, the architects were instructed to model it on the building of St Basil's Cathedral opposite. Consequently, the edifice, which was erected on the original site of Moscow's first university, was decorated with a wide variety of design features. The building itself is now one of the city's main architectural highlights.

Moscow's National Museum

The ornately decorated interior contains almost 45,000 exhibits of Russian history, which bring alive the country's development from the early beginnings of the Kievan Rus, through the period of the Tatars and Tsars and finally to the October Revolution.

The 48 rooms can only display a fraction of an enormous collection of over 4.5 million exhibits. Most of these came into the museum's possession after having been confiscated

by the state following the October Revolution.

Impressive view of the past

One of the building's most notable features is that even the rear elevation of the building is arrestingly beautiful. The Historical Museum separates Red Square from Manege Square. The rear view is consequently just as conspicuously on show as its front elevation. The building is slightly less ornate on this side, however, and its lines are more clearly defined.

A large memorial stands in front of the museum: a statue depicting Georgi Zhukov on horseback, a legendary general of the Soviet army. It was he who stopped the German army's advance in World War II, captured Berlin, and received the German surrender. This military commander, who later fell out of favor, is portrayed pointing the way forward

while his horse is trampling on the swastika and imperial German eagle.

Entrance to Red Square

To the side of the Historical Museum—toward the Church of the Virgin of Kazan—is the impressive Resurrection Gate. Architecturally speaking, it forms part of the Historical Museum. This large construction is characterized by two pointed towers, topped by Russian two-headed eagles.

This gate was a victim of Stalin's mania for destruction. The building, which was first built in the 16th century, was rebuilt in its original form during the 1990s. Nowadays, the double gateway forms the dividing point between the bustling city and the pedestrianized Red Square.

The rear of the Historical Museum is just as impressive as its main façade. The equestrian monument features Georgi Zhukov, who defeated the Germans during World War II (above).

The large red brick building divides Red Square from the city. It adjoins the Resurrection Gate that forms the main entrance to this famous square.

Russia's largest church

The Cathedral of Christ the Savior, rebuilt in 1997, is a new building incorporating an underground garage and restaurant

LOCATION:
Uliza Volchonka

OPENING TIMES:
Daily 10 a.m.-6 p.m.

GETTING THERE:
Metro: Kropotkinskaya

Russian rulers have always erected monuments to themselves—regardless of whether they were Tsars or Patriarchs, provincial princes or city regents. If it were not for these monuments, Russia would not be one of the world's most famous cultural centers.

This need for recognition has not diminished in any way—Moscow's representatives, Mayor Yuri Lushkov in particular, remain committed to this tradition. He had a huge monument erected to Peter the Great and ordered the rebuilding of the Cathedral of Christ the Savior—Russia's largest and most modern church.

To the west of the Kremlin, right on the Moskva, this gigantic church soars above the rooftops of the city—on the very spot that the original church once stood, built between 1838 and 1888 to commemorate the Russian victory over Napoleon. The building with its 338-ft (103-m) high domed tower was the work of the famous architect Konstantin Thon and was in its day the most ambitious, most magnificent and most expensive building project in the city's history. The gold cupolas alone were decorated with 937lbs (425kg) of gold.

A thorn in the side of the Soviet state

After the October Revolution, however, the very monumentality of the cathedral as a prominent symbol of the Orthodox faith led to its own downfall. As far as Stalin was concerned, it was a thorn in the side of the new Socialist Russia and in 1931 the dictator quite simply had the church demolished without further ado.

In its place arose the gigantic building of the Palace of the Soviets, a symbol of the new spirit and a demonstration of Soviet power. Stalin is reputed to have utilized the pillars of the demolished cathedral in building the university and its marble in the metro.

The dictator's plans came to grief, however, initially as a result of weak foundations. Technical problems, as well as the Soviet Union's involvement in World War II, meant that work on the palace had to be suspended and plans for the gigantic project conceived by the late Soviet leader, who died in 1953, eventually fizzled out.

Instead, the large exposed area in the middle of Moscow was utilized in 1960 for another major project: the world's largest swimming-pool. When its poor state of repair led to its closure in 1993, the Russian-Orthodox Church, by now enjoying a revival, laid claim to its former property and the rebuilding of the Cathedral of Christ the Savior got underway.

The distinctive and majestic, newly restored Cathedral of Christ the Savior occupies a commanding position on the banks of the Moskva river (facing page).

Inside the church, its impressive 338-ft (103-m) high dome is decorated in the classical style (left).

The Cathedral is brightly illuminated after dusk, and is one of Moscow's most attractive sights by night (below).

Evidence of a new era

Mayor Yuri Lushkov regarded the restoration of the Cathedral as a prestigious project and a "symbol of Russia's spiritual and moral rebirth." He worked untiringly to get financial support for its reconstruction and personally collected over 200 million dollars in private donations.

Thanks to these efforts, the foundation stone for the new church was laid on January 7, 1995, by Patriarch Alexey II. The building was completed on schedule just four years later to coincide with the city's 850th anniversary. It took a further two years, however, before the final fresco was in place.

The new church is not an identical copy of the original, but is, in many respects, a remarkable modern building. Inside this imposing church, for example, the names of fallen soldiers can be found engraved in alabaster alongside the names of its sponsors. Beneath the building is an underground car park with access to the sanctuary, a bakery for consecrated bread, as well as a museum and restaurant.

The tower commands amazing views from the dome over the city, an experience which is only available as part of a guided tour.

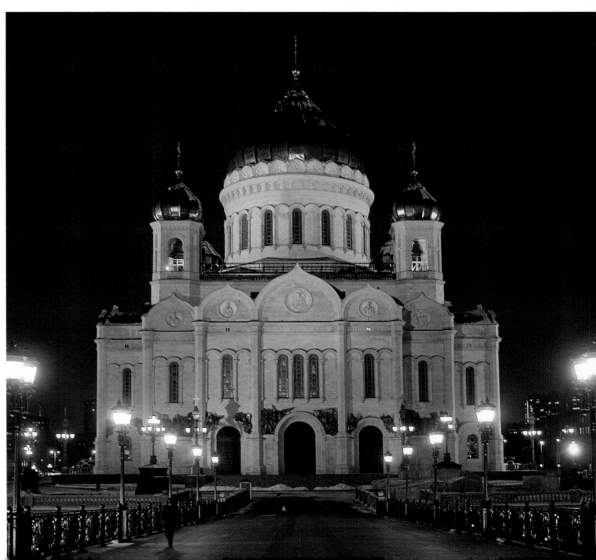

A city of churches and monasteries

In addition to its cultural-heritage sites and world-famous attractions, Moscow is rich in fascinating and treasured religious buildings

church of the monastery, the Church of the Assumption. Efforts are also underway meanwhile to restore the entire complex, the main façade of which is a masterpiece of old-style Russian architecture.

Fairy-tale church

At the other end of the city, a delightful cathedral-style church tower is waiting, like Sleeping Beauty, to be awakened from a long sleep: the Church of the Intercession of the Virgin in Fili.

This church, constructed of red tiles and white limestone and topped with gold cupolas rising up into the sky, has a fairytale appearance. No less fascinating is its interior, which is dominated by wood-carvings by master craftsmen and an extremely valuable iconostasis.

These are just a few examples of the diversity of fascinating churches to be found within Moscow's city boundaries. When visiting the city, pushing open the doors of one of the less well-known churches to enjoy the splendor and mystique of these religious buildings will almost always turn out to be a rewarding experience.

The Church of the Intercession of the Virgin in Fili has a fairy-tale appearance (facing page).

The small Trinity Church, like so many other churches in Moscow, is just waiting to be discovered (left).

The Krutitskiy monastery residence was once described as a small paradise (below).

Whether sandwiched between tall skyscrapers, standing isolated by the side of a busy thoroughfare, crouched behind heavy building site fences, standing alone in the middle of an area of green, hidden behind monastery walls or majestically crowning a hilltop, wherever you go in Moscow, you will come across romantic little chapels, richly decorated churches and even cathedral-style religious buildings. Even though the dark period of Soviet rule wiped out countless churches, Moscow is and remains a city of churches and monasteries.

Rewarding voyages of discovery

Anyone setting out on a journey of discovery is bound to come across architectural treasures. While other places would be vaunting such treasures, guidebooks to Moscow and informational pamphlets are largely devoid of any mention of them. More often than not, they do not even contain the names of these religious gems.

In addition to its numerous churches, Moscow also has a wealth of monastery complexes, particularly in the outer suburbs. In times past, they must have stood alone as protective defensive outposts, but now they have been swallowed up by the enormous spread of urban growth until they are

now almost on the point of being eclipsed altogether. Consequently, visitors will need to look hard and invest a generous amount of time to locate and explore the most culturally important of them. Such efforts will prove very rewarding—as in the case of the Weber Church, for example, not far from the Kremlin, or the Trinity Church of Nikitniki in the city center.

A monastery paradise

Farther outside the city, many metro stations removed from the Kremlin, you will encounter larger churches and monasteries such as the Krutitskiy monastery on the Moskva river. This monastery, built on a small rise in the 13th century, was later to play a role in the writing of ecclesiastical history. In the 16th and 17th centuries, the Metropolitan of the Danube region had his seat here. During the monastery's heyday, this must have been one of the most spectacular places in Russia.

Downfall under Catherine

All this changed when Catherine the Great came to power. She disbanded the monastery and the Soviets hammered the final nail in the coffin. The Communists used the site as a barracks and a prison. Nowadays, services are once again held in the central

Russia's temple to art

The famous Tretyakov Gallery opens up a fascinating window onto Russian art history

Moscow
Russia

LOCATION:
Lavrushinskiy
Pereulok 10

OPENING TIMES:
Daily 10 a.m.–7.30 p.m.,
closed Monday

GETTING THERE:
Metro: Tretyakovksaya,
Polyanka

The Tretyakov Gallery houses an exhibition of Russian painting from the 11th to the 20th century, including many masterpieces unknown in the West.

If there is one single museum in Moscow which is a "must" to visit, then it is the Tretyakov Gallery: not only is it Moscow's largest museum but it is regarded as the most important of its kind anywhere in the world.

The museum has over 100,000 of its own art works on display, all by exclusively Russian and Soviet artists and ranging from medieval paintings to 20th-century sculpture. This vast classical-style collection of buildings in the south of Moscow is most famous, however, for what is undoubtedly the world's largest and most valuable collection of icons. Visiting the treasures of the Tretyakov Gallery is like opening up a richly illustrated picture book of Russian art history.

Pavel's legacy

The museum owes its name to Pavel Tretyakov, whose villa now forms the heart of the museum. He was the son of a rich Muscovite family and was more interested in art than in his father's textile factory. In 1856, this

young merchant bought *The Temptation*, a work by Nikolaus Schilder, thereby marking the birth of what was to become Moscow's most famous museum.

Pavel invested more and more of his wealth in contemporary modern art. He soon found it necessary to build an extension onto his villa to accommodate the enormous number of masterpieces he had begun to accumulate.

From private collection to major art museum

What began as a haphazard collection of artworks grew, with the help of artist Ilya Repin, into a comprehensive exhibition of Russian art. Repin is regarded as one of the most significant realists of Russian painting. His works include outstanding pieces dedicated to Russian history.

In 1874, Pavel Tretyakov decided to make his life's work accessible to the public. Shortly afterward, this merchant, who dedicated his life to art, transferred his entire collection to a museum, thereby handing over 2,000 paintings and sculptures to the city of Moscow. He did, of course, continue to run the museum himself.

Even though the gallery had already achieved its reputation as an important museum during the lifetime of its founder, it was not until after the October Revolution that it gained international significance. The Soviets concentrated their collection of major art works from all over the country here. The number of masterpieces which form part of what is now known as the "Tretyakov Museum Collection" greatly swelled as a result of the state's appropriation of private and ecclesiastical treasures.

The most important icon collection in the world

This state theft resulted in the world's most significant collection of icons. These great religious treasures of the Russian Orthodox Church, including, in pride of place, the "Virgin of Vladimir," the most famous icon in all Russia, are housed in a special section for visitors to marvel over. This is not the only reason for visiting the Tretyakov Gallery, as it is once again known, however: since 1995, more than 60 rooms have been completely renovated and now display masterpieces of painting from the 11th to the 20th century. These include works by painters, such as Alexander Ivanov, who have remained largely unknown in the West.

Outside the entrance to the museum stands a monument to Pavel Tretyakov, the museum's founder. The bust depicting this great patron of the arts is the work of Moscow sculptor Alexander Kibalnikov.

The rooms of this famous museum were completely renovated during the 1990s and reorganized by subject.

The icons on display here are among Russia's most valuable cultural treasures. They were all formerly owned by the Church and confiscated by the Soviets after the October Revolution.

Looking westward

The Pushkin Museum plays host to Western art from classical times to the modern era

LOCATION:
Volkhonka 12

OPENING TIMES:
Daily 10 a.m.-7 p.m.,
Closed Monday

INTERNET:
www.museum.ru

GETTING THERE:
Metro: Kropotkinskaya,
Aleksandrovskiy Sad
Borovitskaya

Classical Roman and Greek statutes once formed the core of the original Museum of Fine Arts collection. They are displayed both inside as well as outside the building (below).

Since the days of Peter the Great, the Russian people have looked with great longing toward the West, a part of the world that was unattainably distant for most people yet incredibly fascinating from a cultural point of view. The Pushkin Museum of Fine Arts, more than anywhere else in Moscow, enabled people to indulge this yearning. This was especially true during the Soviet era, when this world-famous collection provided the sole opportunity to experience Western and, in particular, French art and culture, so popular with the Russian people.

The Pushkin Museum, an extremely rich and remarkable building officially known as the "State Museum of Fine Arts A.S. Pushkin," is situated on Volkhonka Street, a few steps away from the Kremlin's Borovitsky Gate Tower, the Cathedral of Christ the Savior and the Lenin Library. This representational, neoclassical building houses a large collection of important works by many West European artists—both originals and copies.

Ideology through art

When the Pushkin Museum was founded in 1912 with the help of financial donations, it was originally intended solely to exhibit copies of famous paintings from all cultures and periods of art. The aim was to provide students of the Academy of Art History with an authentic view of Western art history. Since those early days, how-ever, the collection has grown to number over 1,000 copies and originals, comprising antiquities from the Middle East, Egypt, Greece, and the Byzantine Empire, as well as classical and Renaissance works. These include

The magnificent neo-classical architecture of the Pushkin Museum complements the sumptuous artwork on display as part of its classical collection.

Its outstanding collection of Impressionist works has earned the Pushkin Museum its international reputation (below).

plaster casts of originals, accurate to the smallest detail, such as the Pharaoh's sarcophagus and Michelangelo's David.

The museum's importance increased after the October Revolution: as privately owned collections were confiscated by the state, a considerable number of artworks fell into the hands of Moscow's museums. In line with its original concept, the Pushkin Museum concentrated on non-Russian and non-Soviet art. Later, it absorbed the collections of French Impressionist and Cubist works belonging to the Moscow Museum of Modern Western Art following the latter's closure after World War II.

The French works on display at the Pushkin Museum today include major paintings by classicists such as David, Fragonard, Watteau, Poussin; the Impressionist painters Cézanne, Manet, Monet; and modernists such as Matisse. Italian painters, including Botticelli, Perugino, and Tiepolo, as well as Spaniards such as El Greco, Murillo, Vélazquez, Zurbarán, and Picasso are generously represented. Among its collection, the museum also includes paintings by Flemish painters such as Rubens, Jordaens, and Van Dyk and the Dutch masters Rembrandt, De Hooc, and Van Gogh.

The Priamos Treasure

The Pushkin Museum houses a permanent special exhibition in its seventh hall, which includes one of the world's greatest treasures: the treasure of Priamos, lost without trace for many years and steeped in legend. Also known as the gold of Troy, the centerpiece of this cultural treasure is the great diadem created from pure gold and crafted over 4,500 years ago from 16,337 individual parts.

As in all great museums of the world, the Pushkin Museum can only display a fraction of its collection in the exhibition halls. It does, however, stage a continuous succession of brilliant and comprehensive special events highlighting specific periods of art, individual artists or series of paintings. In doing so, its directors constantly manage to surprise the art world. For this reason alone, visits to this wonderful museum will always be worthwhile on each fresh occasion.

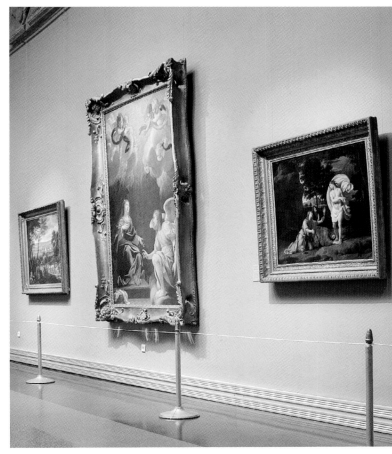

Memorial to a writer and thinker

The Maxim Gorky Museum in the Ryabushinsky Villa is among the most beautiful museums dedicated to Moscow's writers

asymmetrical wall projections, encircling mosaic frieze and variously shaped balconies defining it from the architectural uniformity that surrounds it.

Spectacular staircase

The main highlight of the building is the centrally located stairwell with its unique twisting staircase, illuminated by a richly decorated glass roof that tapers to a point.

The entire interior was personally designed by Shekhtel and conceived as part of an artistic ensemble with every object, from lamp to fireplace, decorated with the recurring laurel-leaf motif. In this respect the Villa Ryabushinsky is an outstanding example of Art Nouveau architecture—also known as "Modern Style."

As is usual in Moscow, this private house, which once belonged to the famous artist and revolutionary "Model Writer" Maxim Gorky, is open to the public as a museum. He also spent some time in the West—Italy and Germany in particular—and the museum, which contains over 12,000 books and many original drawings, provides a glimpse of the writer's life and his private library.

LOCATION:
Malaya Nikitskaya Uliza 6/2

OPENING TIMES:
Daily 12 a.m.-6.30 p.m., Closed Monday

GETTING THERE:
Metro: Arbatskaya Pushkinskaya

The twisting staircase is one of the villa's architectural highlights (opposite).

This bust of Gorky now stands in his living-room (left).

Gorky's villa is a perfect example of the Russian "Modern Style" (below).

One of the most surprising aspects of the Russian soul is the honor this nation bestows on its most prominent writers and thinkers, not to mention its composers, musicians and performing artists. Whereas in most other cultural capitals of the world, one is more likely to encounter statues of famous rulers or military generals, in Moscow the visitor will come across portraits of world-famous writers and thinkers such as Tolstoy, Pushkin, and Gorky displayed in numerous locations.

Every young child of primary school age will be familiar with their names—partly because museum visits form an integral part of their education. In this way, the children not only get to know the major art galleries, but also become familiar with the small but excellent museums which are dedicated to prominent cultural figures. One is the Tolstoy Museum, situated in the heart of the city.

The most beautiful of these memorial buildings from an architectural point of view is, without doubt, the Maxim Gorky Museum in the Ryabushinsky Villa, the so-called Shekhtel House, which is one of the most outstanding examples of an Art Nouveau building in the world.

In 1931 at Stalin's behest, this architectural treasure was handed over to Maxim Gorky, who spent the last five years of his life in the house. At the time this detached mansion close to the city center was an intellectual hub and meeting-place for international writers and politicians, including many visitors from overseas.

Intricate decoration

The villa was built at the beginning of the 20th century for the Moscow millionaire banker and merchant Ryabushinsky by the architect Fyodor Shekhtel, who saw the building as an artistic ensemble, richly ornamented both inside and out and decorated with a recurring motif of laurel leaves.

The building is an unmistakable landmark of urban architecture, its

Russia's prima ballerina

The Bolshoi Theater is known as the home of the world's best ballet company as well as Moscow's oldest theater

LOCATION:
Theatralnaya Square 1

INFO HOTLINE:
+7 495 / 292 99 86
10 a.m.-7 p.m.

BOX OFFICE TELEPHONE:
+7 495 / 250 73 17
10 a.m.-7 p.m.

GETTING THERE:
Metro: Theatralnaya,
Okhotny Ryad

OPENING TIMES:
Main box office: daily
New Theater Box Office:
Tues.-Sun. 11 a.m.-7 p.m.

INTERNET:
www.bolshoi.ru/en/

Bolshoi—the very name will give ballet lovers and culture enthusiasts worldwide a thrill. It is the epitome of top-class ballet and Russia's biggest cultural export. Even during the Soviet era, when Russians were rarely allowed to leave the country, Bolshoi dancers performed all over the world. They were among the very few artists allowed to represent Russian culture abroad during the Soviet period.

The ballet company's home is the Bolshoi Theater in Moscow. This classical-style building is an architectural highlight in the city and one of the most beautiful theaters in the world.

Its international reputation is symbolized by the bronze quadriga, which crowns the building. Its creator, Petr Klodt, depicted Apollo, god of the arts and light, drawing the sun from the heavens.

The Bolshoi Theater can boast a history reaching back 200 years. Since its foundation, it has been destroyed by fire and rebuilt several times. In 1776, the Tsar granted Prince Urussov the exclusive right to stage dramas and operas in Moscow, whereupon, in 1780, the prince commissioned the theater to be built on its present site. The façade of the building overlooked Petrovka Street and consequently

became known as the Petrovkiy Theater. In those days it was the prince's bondsmen who performed and sang on the stage—signaling the birth of the ballet. In 1825, after the theater was destroyed by fire, court architect Osip Bove built a new theater on the same site. Twenty-five years later this building also burnt down. The present Bolshoi Theater building was finally built in 1825 and follows a classical design by the Italian architect Alberto Cavos. The façade is dominated by eight magnificent pillars and crowned by the Apollo quadriga.

Behind the pillars, two massive wooden doors open on to a white

The Bolshoi Ballet has thrilled audiences for decades with its unchanging sets, including Tchaikovsky's Nutcracker Suite. These sets have become as famous as the pieces themselves (right).

marble foyer embellished with gold. The auditorium can seat an audience of 2,300 people in five tiers, in the center of which is the Tsar's sumptuous royal box. The splendor of this theater positively breathes history: great Russian names such as Rubinstein, Tchaikovsky, Rachmaninov, and famous foreign artists, such as Richard Wagner, have all performed here.

During the 1920s and 30s, the Bolshoi focused on ballet, becoming the best classical dance company in the world. Since then it has continued to enjoy great success, thrilling audiences with ballets such as "Swan Lake," which have remained unchanged for decades. Perhaps its success lies in the fact that it embodies the contradicting characteristics of the Russian soul: heavy and light, Orthodox and atheist, exuberant and graceful.

The magical set of Swan Lake can be seen in guest performances all over the world (above).

The bronze quadriga by sculptor Petr Klodt on the roof of the Bolshoi Theater depicts Apollo, the god of the muse, in his sun chariot.

The magnificent boulevards

The Old Arbat and the Tverskaya Uliza are where Moscow's pulse beats in the shadow of historic façades

GETTING THERE:
ARBAT:
Metro: Arbatskaya,
Smolenskaya

TVERSKAYA ULIZA:
Metro: Tverskaya,
Mayakovskaya,
Okhotny Ryad

If you ask a Muscovite what the city's main sights are—apart from the Kremlin and the cathedrals—you will almost certainly be pointed in the direction of the Old Arbat and Tverskaya Uliza. Both these magnificent boulevards are packed with historic splendor. More importantly, however, they are the pride of modern Moscow—places where you will find the finest coffee houses and best shops, the most popular restaurants and many of the top hotels.

The two thoroughfares could not be more different, however: whereas the Arbat, the city's first pedestrianized zone with its souvenir shops and street vendors trading before a backdrop of magnificent villas, is mainly a tourist magnet heavy, the Tverskaya Uliza is a six-lane highway dominated by traffic. Nevertheless, it does provide a more authentic impression of life in the metropolis and the bustle of modern Moscow.

The Old Arbat

During the 15th century, the Arbat district was populated by Asian settlers who gave the area its name, which is derived from the Arabic *rabat*. The district's main street formed the main trade route between the Kremlin and Smolensk.

During the first half of the 19th century, this quarter was the domain of artists, literary figures, actors and merchants with their stalls and stores. The local theater is still associated with such great figures as Gogol, Tolstoy, Tchaikovsky and Repin. The Arbat was also home to one of the intellectual cells which led to the October Revolution.

The echoes of famous artists are still evident: Pushkin had an apartment in the elegant sky-blue mansion known as "Palais Khitrovo" at Arbat 55. Tchaikovsky also lived for a time in this house, which now houses a Pushkin Museum. Next door is the house where writer Andrei Bely lived; it too is now a public museum.

The magnificent house of Constructivist Konstantin Melnikov in a side street of Krivoarbatskiy Pereulok, Old Arbat, is a "must-see" for visitors. It is shaped in the form of two interlocking cylinders that form a circular structure. The façade is punctuated with honeycomb-shaped windows.

Even today, the streets of Old Arbat are still peopled with artists, either drawing charcoal portraits, making scissor silhouettes of predominantly foreign visitors, or selling watercolor or oil paintings of Moscow's main sights which are popular as tourist souvenirs.

Tverskaya Uliza

Built in the 14th century as a road linking Moscow with Tver, the Tverskaya Uliza was the first paved road in Moscow. Peter the Great used it to move from his old capital to his new capital city. During the 18th century, it became popular among elegant Russian social circles as a desirable place to live. Lined with distinctive buildings, it had become, prior to the October Revolution, Moscow's most magnificent boulevard.

The arrival of Stalin, however, brought an abrupt end to the glamor. He had the road, which he renamed after Maxim Gorky, widened to 12ft (4m) to accommodate his parades. Only a fraction of the historic buildings were "moved"—many more were simply demolished. Despite this, the boulevard still boasts many remarkable buildings, including the Hotel National, the Yermolova Theater, Moscow City Hall, and the former Hotel Lux, a fine example of Art Nouveau architecture. Pushkin Square, in the center of which is a large monument to the writer, is part way along Tverskaya Street.

One of the indisputable highlights of this boulevard is Yeliseyev's, the famous old Moscow delicatessen. The inside of the store is ornately decorated in stucco work and gold leaf, more reminiscent of a palace than a store. Shopping here will give the visitor a taste of how truly sumptuous the Tverskaya Uliza boulevard was in its heyday.

The rich ornamentation (above) on some of the magnificent buildings on Tverskaya Uliza reflects how elegant this boulevard must once have appeared. Sadly, many of its distinctive buildings were destroyded during Stalin's era.

The interior of Yeliseyev's Delicatessen is more like a palace than a store (opposite, bottom).

The Khitrovo House in the Arbat has been turned into a museum to Pushkin even though he only lived here for a short time after his marriage (left).

Stalin's confectionery

The first skyscrapers to dominate the silhouette of Moscow's skyline are known as the "seven sisters"

HOTEL UKRAINIA:
Kutusovskiy Prospect
2/1

HOTEL LENINGRADSKAYA:
Kalanchevskaya Uliza
21/40

**MINISTRY OF FOREIGN
AFFAIRS:**
Smolenskaya Ploshad

**LOMONOSOV UNIVER-
SITY:**
Lomonosovskiy
Prospect

**MINISTRY FOR HEAVY
INDUSTRY:**
Sadovaya-Spasskaya
Uliza 21

APARTMENT BUILDING:
Kudrinskaya Ploshad

APARTMENT BUILDING:
Kotelnicheskaya
Naberezhnaya

**Outside the city gates is
the tallest of the seven
sisters–Lomonosov
University (below).**

In 1933, Stalin had a vision: in the same way that American skyscrapers embody capitalism, a new style of architecture should be created in Moscow that would attest to the greatness of socialism and reflect its spirit.

It was not until 1947, however, that the state government issued the decree ordering the erection of appropriate skyscrapers. The decree claimed that the proportions and silhouettes of these buildings were to be original and their architectural and artistic composition were to be compatible with the city's existing historic architecture and the future silhouette of the planned Palace of Soviets. The decree continued accordingly, the skyscrapers should not replicate the sort of skyscrapers we are familiar with in other countries.

The result is a unique type of skyscraper featuring numerous superstructures, towers, turrets and decorations. Cultural critics in the West, however, where the emphasis already lay on clear, simple lines, were generally disparaging, remarking that the buildings had a "confectionery style." Nevertheless, these buildings exercise the same sort of fascination as did the ones in major U.S. cities in their day.

At the center of this new group of buildings was to be the Palace of Soviets, which would determine the location, height and shape of the skyscrapers. These monumental buildings were erected in designated squares according to strategic considerations as with a fortification system. In doing so, the architects were given free rein to raze any building they deemed unnecessary to the ground. The result was an irreplaceable loss of culturally significant buildings.

The project to build the gigantic palace foundered, however, when it was found impossible to meet all the structural engineering requirements. Instead, eight high-rise buildings were designed in 1947 to mark the coming 800th anniversary of the city. Seven of these were erected in the years that followed: the University, the Ministry of Foreign Affairs, two administrative buildings and two apartment blocks, as well as a hotel.

Since this time, these symbols of Soviet self-esteem have dominated the city skyline like the peaks of a high mountain. They are visible from every part of Moscow. The country's most renowned architects were commissioned with their design. Modeled on American skyscrapers from the 1920s and 1930s, the steel framework structures were clad with bricks and finished with natural stone slabs. It took just four years to construct these huge buildings. This was only possible, however, by conscripting whole armies of forced labor.

The tallest and most important was Lomonossov University at Sparrow Hills. Compared with the many new high-rise buildings, this structure is relatively small and for this reason, locals no longer speak of the "seven sisters," but refer to them scornfully as the "seven dwarfs."

The Ministry of Foreign Affairs is housed in one of the skyscrapers intended to embody Stalin's vision of a new style of architecture. The building was designed down to the minutest detail and furnished with an individual style of décor. Western architectural critics were contemptuous of the style, which they referred to—unfairly—as "confectionery." The "seven sisters" command a similar degree of fascination as the Western skyscrapers of the same period.

The halls of commerce

The All-Russian Exhibition Center in Moscow is one of the most beautiful exhibition grounds in the world. It once represented the pride of the Soviet Republics

LOCATION:
GAO VVC, Estate 118, Prospect Mira

OPENING TIMES:
May–October: 10 a.m.-6 p.m., Sat and Sun 10 a.m.-7 p.m.;
November–April: 10 a.m.-5 p.m., Sat and Sun 10 a.m.-6 p.m.

GETTING THERE:
Metro: WDNCh; Bus: 33, 56, 76, 93, 136, 154, 172, 195, 239, 244, 803;
Trolley bus: 14, 48, 76;
Tram: 11, 17

The Soviet leadership was always very sure of itself and its economic achievements. It is hardly surprising, therefore, that soon after the October Revolution an arena was created to prove to themselves, their own citizens, and the rest of the world just what they were capable of: the All-Russian Exhibition Center.

Russia in miniature

A Russia in miniature was presented to the world on a golden platter: 72 Stalinist exhibition palaces displayed collections from industry, science and culture for visitors to marvel over. They came from every region and land within the Soviet Republic. After World War II, the exhibition grounds were extended even further to encompass architecture, painting, film and music, which all combined to create one single artistic whole, a symbol of the Soviet dream.

A vast avenue leads to Pavilion No. 1, a 318-ft (97-m) tall, confectionery-style "Cathedral." Nearby is Kolchose Square with its Friendship of Nations fountain, the most spectacular of its kind in Moscow. It features 15 gilded bronze statues of girls

wearing the national costumes of the Union Republics grouped around a water feature fed by 800 fountains.

The center is comprised of 16 pavilions dedicated to the individual Union Republics and decorated in a manner traditional to each region: the Siberian pavilion, for example is decorated with pine cones, the Ukraine pavilion resembles a granary, while the Moscow pavilion contains a miniature Kremlin.

A particular attraction for visitors was and still is the "Pavilion of Space," which contains models of Sputnik satellites, spacesuits and sections of Soyuz rockets. Visitors can also marvel at the outstanding scientific achievements that enabled the legend of space travel, Yuri Gagarin, to be the first man in space.

From spectacle to fair

The winds of change which blew away the old Soviet state likewise affected the All-Russian Exhibition Center—nowadays it is no longer the Soviet Republics which are represented there, but international companies. The area is now home to the VVC, the Moscow Fair, welcoming manufactur-

ers and visitors to this extraordinary exhibition center, which has no equal anywhere in the world. It understandably attracts great interest since Moscow plays a key role in Russia's economy and around 80 percent of the country's financial potential is concentrated here. Consequently, the All-Russian Exhibition Center is one of the most important commercial centers in Rusia.

Added to this is the fact that the Moscow region is the country's most important industrial center, responsible for 60 percent of all foreign investments.

The area represents, however, far more than just traditional exhibition grounds—it is also doubles as an amusement park with landscaped gardens.

Moscow's All-Russian Exhibition Center is one of the most beautiful exhibition sites in the world.

Every pavilion is individually designed and elaborately decorated (opposite).

The Friendship of Nations fountain features bronze statues, whose dance around the fountains symbolizes the Union of the Soviet Republics (left).

Subterranean art

The Moscow Metro stations are miniature art galleries: each one is individually designed and ornately decorated

METRO SYSTEM:
179 miles (276km), 12 lines

STATIONS:
170 stations, 22 underground

CAPACITY:
Transports approximately 10 million people a day

The décor at Kievskaya Station transfigures Soviet daily life in lavish mosaics (right).

The architecture of Mayakovskaya Station was awarded the Grand Prix at the New York World Fair (above far right).

The bronze brigadists at "Revolution Square" Station are portrayed in militant attitude (below).

The escalator plunges in breathtaking fashion down into the depths of the earth. As you step onto the ceaselessly moving staircase, the end of it can only be imagined rather than actually seen. Masses of people bunch together, waiting in line to embark. Packed together, yet briskly moving and very disciplined—this is the Moscow subway.

A train passes through every 20 seconds yet even so, people are packed like sardines during *chas pik*, rush hour. Sometimes there is simply no room to fit into the packed carriages.

Journey into the past

For Muscovites, a Metro trip is always a journey into the past. "Revolution Square" station provides an initial foretaste of this underground art world, which spans 11 historic stations over 155 miles (250 km) of track.

Bearded soldiers, sailors, and farmers cast in bronze, stretch their rifles and revolvers toward the Metro travelers; the half-crouching, almost kneeling, grim-faced revolutionaries are a reminder of the era of Revolution.

Construction work on the metro began on Stalin's orders in the 1930s and the Metro construction workers sang "Faster and faster, farther and farther, higher and higher," as they toiled.

In building this transport system, the Soviet Union, as the first state to anchor atheism in its constitution,

turned its attention to the religious legacies of ancient cultures. Long stretches of the Metro resemble an underground temple system. Sometimes it feels as though one has been transported to the Roman catacombs. The stations are often extravagantly decorated in marble, granite, semiprecious stones and fitted with crystal chandeliers.

Symbols of Soviet culture

The station décor frequently exhibits symbols of Soviet culture, including the hammer and sickle and five-pronged star. Artists also introduced mosaics depicting ancient symbols, cabbalist motifs and even runes. Occasionally, you may feel as though you have strayed into an ancient civilization; for example, at Kropotkinskaya Station, beautifully designed lamps illuminate a double colonnade of columns that resemble an Egyptian temple. All that is missing are the actual torches.

Prize-winning architecture

The farther one travels away from the center with its lavishly decorated stations and into the suburbs, the simpler the décor becomes. Only in the center of the city will you encounter entrance buildings above ground—structures that often resemble mausoleums. The Soviet leader Lenin's final resting-place was used to advantage in this way—the Metro was named after him.

By far the most beautiful of all the Metro stations, Mayakovksaya Station, is also the deepest underground. Its simple yet remarkably elegant architecture was awarded one of the main prizes at the New York World Fair in 1938. It is also a significant historical site: when the Germans were at the gates of Moscow in 1942, Stalin had the Revolution celebrations held here.

The golden convent

The Tsars frequently banished their unwanted wives to the magnificent New Virgin Nunnery

Moscow
Russia

LOCATION:
Novodevichy Proesd 1

OPENING TIMES:
Daily 8 a.m.–5 p.m.,
Closed Tuesday

SERVICES:
Daily 8 a.m. and 5 p.m.,
except Sun

GETTING THERE:
Metro: Sportivnaya

The New Virgin Nunnery is one of the most beautiful collections of buildings in Moscow and is internationally recognized as a gem of cultural history.

A prison as a cultural heritage site

The pleasant-sounding name of this UNESCO World Heritage site effectively disguises the fact that this mighty complex—which is surrounded by thick walls—was in fact once used as a prison for wives. The Tsars, when they had tired of their wives, simply banished them to the Novodevichy Convent so that they would be free to look for a new woman.

The first Tsarist wife to suffer this fate was Sophia, half-sister of Peter I. A few years later, Peter's wife likewise found herself incarcerated in this convent, which is why the abbots were constantly being granted gifts of land. During its heyday, the convent commanded around 15,000 serfs who worked on its farms.

The convent as a fortress

The complex was originally designed during the 16th century as a fortified nunnery, built to stop further incursions by the Lithuanians and Crimean Tatars. When the Crimean Tatar Khan, Mehmet Girai, marched on Moscow in 1571 the New Virgin Nunnery was unable to offer him any effective resistance. Newly built, however, the final assault by the heathen Tatars was successfully repelled in 1591.

After his victory over Smolensk in 1514, Vassily III commissioned the Cathedral of the Virgin of Smolensk.

Its design strongly suggests the influence of Italian architects in its construction. Its builders added new elements such as covered galleries. The Cathedral of the Annunciation likewise reveals similar design elements.

Inside the building, the first thing to catch the eye is the gilded five-tiered iconostasis, donated by the unfortunate Sophia, who commissioned craftsmen to create it in 1683. The frescoes depict Smolensk's annexation to the Russian Empire. Also displayed on the wall is the icon of the Virgin of Smolensk, which is reputed to have miraculous powers.

The main hall, situated in the refectory, comprises an area of $4,200\text{ft}^2$ (390m^2). Not only did it serve the nuns as a dining hall, but it was also used to receive important guests such as the Tsar. The 236 ft (72 m) high bell tower is six stories high and richly decorated with ornate window projections, balustrades and pillars.

Famous graves

The convent's famous cemetery is also worth a visit. It was created at the end of the 19th century as a final resting place for the city's rich, famous and beautiful. For a long time, however, the many lavishly decorated graves of famous figures such as Gogol, Chekhov, Tolstoy and Tretyakov were out of bounds to visitors. The reason being that Nikita Khrushchev is buried here—the only Soviet leader not to be interred along the Kremlin Wall as a result of a Politburo decision. His successor, Brezhnev, closed the cemetery to visitors in an attempt to discourage disagreeable demonstrations.

The grave of controversial Party Secretary Nikita Khrushchev features black and white marble as a symbol of the good and bad sides to his character (below).

The manner in which Krushchev's widow, Nina Petrovna, marked his memorial is a story in itself. She commissioned the artist Ernst Neisvestny, not one of her husband's favorites, to design a bust of Khrushchev which was then placed between two blocks of marble, one white and one black, to symbolize the General Secretary's good and bad sides.

The gravestones of many of those buried here indicate symbolically how they achieved fame. A statue of a grieving woman has, since 1999, ornamented the grave of the original real First Lady of the Kremlin, Raissa Gorbachev.

The New Virgin Nunnery is picturesquely situated on the banks of the Moskva River a little distance outside the city center. It is listed as a cultural heritage site despite the fact that the Tsars used it as a prison for their wives (above).

In 1581 the Tatars were successfully repelled from the fortified towers of the convent (far left).

Adjoining the Baroque Dormition Chapel is the refectory where the nuns received prominent guests, including the Tsars (left).

"An unparalleled wonder"

The tent-roofed church of Kolomenskoye had a great influence on traditional Russian ecclesiastical architecture

LOCATION:
Proletarskiy Prospect 31

OPENING TIMES:
Museum: 11 a.m.-6 p.m., Closed Mon and Tues; Park: open daily

GETTING THERE:
Metro: Kolomenskaya

Thirty-two year old Sasha generally spends half his day studying historical documents, as befits a historian. However, as soon as the tourist buses start rolling up at St. Savior's Gate just after lunch, Sasha hurries off into the armory of Kolomenskoye Museum and reaches resolutely for his weapons.

Wearing a fur-trimmed cap on his head and sporting the wine-red uniform of a Streltsy guardsman, Sasha strides around the oak woodland of the park, where the Tsar's summer residence was situated during the Middle Ages. This costumed figure, with a halberd and musket casually slung over his shoulder, is quickly surrounded by schoolchildren from nearby Moscow.

On-site history lessons

The Streltsy, Sasha tells the children, were 16th-century guardsmen in the service of Moscow's Grand Princes. They lived in their own districts and because they were so poorly paid, the Tsar allowed them to trade and farm. During the reign of Peter the Great, the Streltsy revolted against their masters, but the uprising was savagely quashed by the Tsar, who then disbanded the Streltsy units.

The historical role of a Streltsy guardsman is not something that Sasha the historian, whose period of military service in the Soviet Army was not an episode he particularly cares to remember, assumes altogether voluntarily. Since his monthly salary can no longer keep pace with the rising cost of living, he charges people to take souvenir photographs of him in uniform in Kolomenskoye park. He also sells miniature clay Streltsy figures to tourists.

An unparalleled wonder

Situated on a hill in the southern part of the city, from where there are superb views across the metropolis, is the Ascension Church, a pure white, stone-built, tent-roofed church, which UNESCO has designated a world heritage site.

The 206-ft (63-m) high church, which has now been fully restored, was built by Grand Prince Ivan III in 1530 to celebrate the long-awaited birth of his son, who was to become known as Ivan the Terrible. Its architecture signified a break with the traditions of the Byzantine style of ecclesiastical architecture. It is of such stunning beauty that the French composer Hector Berlioz described it as "an unparalleled wonder." Almost no other Russian tent-roofed church has had such an influence on sacred architecture throughout eastern Europe as this masterpiece in the old park which used to be the Tsar's sum-

mer resort. It is the only building in the complex to have survived.

The church was ready for dedication after just two years of construction. Despite its impressive external appearance, the interior is relatively modest in size since the walls themselves are up to 13ft (4m) thick. It is plain to see that this building represents the beginning of a new and individual style in Russian ecclesiastical architecture.

Rows of tiles form the tent roof

Three sweeping staircases lead up to the second-story galleries with their picturesque arcades. The 92-ft (28-m) tall tent-like, pointed roof consists of rows of tiles which are tiered inward as the tower narrows to a point. The architects used the structural device of semicircular corbel arches, known as *kokoshniki*, to support the cupola structure, the interior and the tent roof. The roof of the Church of the Ascension also incorporates a room for a guard, whose job it was to alert the watchmen in the Moscow Kremlin's bell tower in the event of approaching Tatar hordes.

The original iconostasis, a wall consisting of three doors, decorated with icons, which separated the sanctuary from the main body of the church, was replaced in the 19th century with a mural from the Ascension Convent in Moscow. All that remains of the original wall are the 16th-century Tsar's doors, which are now on display in a museum within the Kolomenskoye complex.

The famous tent-roofed church is not alone on the hilltop, however, as the complex is also comprised of several other, younger sacred buildings. Entering through the Gate of the Savior one reaches the Church of Our Lady of Kazan, in which regular services are held. Between the two churches is a small museum, housing a model of the Tsar's former palace. Situated a little apart from the Church of the Ascension is the small chapel of St. George with its bell-tower.

Acting extras bring the history of Kolomenskoye alive for tourists (above left).

The mighty Gate of the Savior leads into the park surrounding the former Tsar's palace (above).

While Moscow's older residents enjoy this modern park on the outskirts of the city as a place to stroll, the younger population prefer it as a venue for open-air concerts with views of the modern city skyline (left).

A symphony of wood

Kolomenskoye Park showcases ancient Russian wooden buildings from all over the country

Despite the fact that most Russians have to watch their budget more and more carefully, a visit to the old Tsars' residence remains an integral part of Muscovites' leisure activities, since it is here that some of Old Russia's most beautiful churches and secular buildings are to be found. This park on the outskirts of the busy metropolis of 12 million people is mainly popular with Moscow's younger generation because of its music festival. The park is officially designated a museum complex.

Over the years, people have brought individual sections of demolished bell towers, guardhouses and even an old mead brewery from all over this vast empire into this historical complex, the museum of which has been augmented by the addition of a store selling ceramics, lacquered boxes, textiles, and wooden household items from the Chochloma workshops. One of the loveliest wooden churches to be moved to this site is the Church of Our Lady of Kazan. This building, topped by two onion-shaped domes, was built in the 17th century.

Memories of Tsar Peter

In tribute to the memory of Peter the Great, building workers reassembled a small wooden house that the Tsar had inhabited on the island of Markov, near Archangelsk.

The Gate Tower of St. Nicholas Convent, built in 1692, once stood by the White Sea in northern Russia.

And the mighty Ostrog, a 17th-century watchtower, was brought by museum staff from Siberia. Individual historical exhibits can also be found in the appropriate section of the Historical Museum.

The former wooden palace, which the Tsars inhabited, no longer exists in its original form. A model of it, complete with tent roofs, onion domes, arcades and balconies, can be viewed in miniature in the Kolomenskoye Museum. Catherine II preferred to spend her summers in her Zarskoye Selo residence near St Petersburg. When this masterpiece of Russian joinery fell into disrepair, she ordered it to be taken down in 1768.

The gate tower from St. Nicholas Monastery, built toward the end of the 17th century, was brought to Kolomenskoye. The church was originally situated on the White Sea coast (opposite and bottom left).

View of the restored wooden chalet where Tsar Peter I stayed during his visit to Archangelsk (left).

Evidence of Old-Russian stone carvings can also be found in Kolomenskoye, an example being the Boris Stone, which once delineated a frontier (bottom right).

A monastery of icons

The history-steeped St Andronikov Monastery is a monument to the icon painter Andrei Rublev

LOCATION:
Andronyevskaya
Ploshchad 10

OPENING TIMES:
Daily 11 a.m.–5 p.m.,
Closed Wednesday

GETTING THERE:
Metro: Ploshchad
Ilyicha

The St Andronikov Monastery is a good indication of how quickly the Russian capital has spread outward and swallowed up more and more of the surrounding area. The monastery, which was founded around 1390 by the monk Andronik, a pupil of St Sergius von Radonezh, is situated in what is now a very busy area. The peaceful and idyllic surroundings, which this place enjoyed in earlier times, has been lost for ever. Stepping through the Holy Gate and entering the compound, however, you will find yourself in an unexpectedly peaceful setings behind the thick defensive walls.

The heroes of Snipe's Field
The monastery played a special role following the battle of Kulikovo Pole, or Snipe's Field, in which the Muscovites, against all predictions to the contrary, forced the Mongolian army to its knees. The fallen warriors were borne back to the capital on biers. Crowds of people descended upon the St Andronikov Monastery to pay them their last respects. The heroes were eventually laid to rest in the monastery's own cemetery.

Since 1947, the monastery has served as a museum of Old Russian history. Its main focus is a collection of icons bearing the name of the

famous icon painter, Andrei Rublev. A memorial to him stands outside the gates to the monastery.

The Archangel Michael and Metropolitan Alexei Church occupies a commanding place on the monastery grounds. When construction on the church began, the monastery was under the patronage of the Lopukhina noble family. Their daughter Yevdokiya was married to Peter I, who later rejected and banished his wife. The Lopukhinas consequently brought construction work on the church to a halt. For almost three decades, the church building remained a ruin. It was not until 1739, 14 years after Peter's death, that it was completed in the Baroque Naryshkin style.

The oldest architectural monument in the monastery complex is the white limestone Cathedral of the Savior. Donated by an affluent Moscow merchant family, this church, once richly decorated in the interior, became a model of Moscow's ecclesiastical architecture. It represents the first time that traditional early Moscow architecture was combined with fresh and dynamic new design elements that were clearly influenced by the Gothic style.

In the middle of the monastery stands the Church of the Archangel Michael and Metropolitan Alexei, the history of which is closely linked to the love life of Peter the Great (above).

The bells, which once again call the faithful to prayer in the Cathedral of the Savior, hang in a wooden, free-standing belfry (opposite).

Behind the walls of the monastery lies the last resting-place of the fallen warriors who vanquished the Tatars and liberated Moscow (left).

The odyssey of the bells

After 70 years, Danilov Monastery has regained its chimes

LOCATION:
Danilovskiy Val

OPENING TIMES:
Daily. 8 a.m.-8 p.m.

GETTING THERE:
Metro: Tulskaya

Founded in 1282, the oldest and biggest cloister in what is now the capital city also boasted the most impressive bell chimes for miles around.

In the wake of the October Revolution, the Soviet government confiscated the Danilov Monastery from the church and used it as a prison. It was later turned into a refrigerator factory. Finally, in 1930, the Soviets sold the monastery's former pride and joy, its 18 bells, to a U.S. industrialist, who gave them to Harvard University, where they hung for many years.

Danilov Monastery was one of the first to be returned by the state to the Orthodox Church. Thus it was—after lengthy negotiations—that 70 years later the bells returned home to their place of origin from across the Atlantic. An exact copy of the Russian originals has chimed at Harvard ever since.

Seat of the Patriarch

Danilov Monastery, which owes its external appearance to architectural monuments of the 17th, 18th and 19th centuries, has been the seat of the Patriarch of Moscow since 1983.

Before this confiscated property was returned to the church, the entire complex was carefully restored by the Russian government.

As a result, these outstanding examples of Russian sacred architecture have been restored to their full splendor. They include the patriarch's cathedral, completed in 1560, the 17th century gateway church, and the Trinity Cathedral, built during the succeeding century.

The Church of the Holy Fathers of the Seven Ecumenical Councils was built in the Danilov Monastery complex in the mid-16th century (opposite).

Danilov, the largest and oldest cloister, also has its own cemetery (above).

The entrance area to the monastery, now the seat of the Patriarch of Moscow, is guarded by a defense tower (left).

A false dream

Catherine wanted a new palace, but the architects' design for Zaryzino did not fit the bill

Moscow
Russia

LOCATION:
Dolskaya Uliza 1, south of the city center near Kolomenskoye

OPENING TIMES:
11 a.m.-4 p.m., Sun 11 a.m.-5 p.m., Closed Mon and Tuesday

GETTING THERE:
Metro: Zarizyno, Orechevo

Situated in the southern part of the city is one of Moscow's most beautiful landscaped parks—Zaryzino. It is the setting for what was to remain the unfulfilled dream of a Tsarina, a fairy-tale palace complex by the same name.

Catherine the Great nurtured the dream of a new fairytale palace for herself—a place of retreat outside the gates of Moscow, which would be modeled on her summer palace outside St Petersburg.

Her attention fell upon a gently hilly region, where Tsarina Irina had already built an estate during the 16th century. She bought the site for 25,000 roubles in 1775 from Prince Kantemir of Moldavia who had acquired the land from Peter the Great.

An ensemble of artistic achievement

This eccentric monarch commissioned Vasily Bayenov, one of the most famous architects of the day, to build the complex. Between 1779 and 1785, he erected a collection of buildings in a pseudo-Gothic style. The royal palace itself was surrounded by red- and white-brick buildings as well as a large number of bridges and pavilions. Bayenov also went to great lengths to include the landscape in his design.

When the Tsarina undertook an inspection tour of the complex, she was horrified. This was not the Zaryzino of her dreams. She was particularly upset by the heavily ornate style of architecture.

Bayenov fell into disgrace and work continued under the supervi-

sion of another architect, Kazakov. When Catherine died in 1797, all work on the project came to a standstill.

In the early 19th century, the complex once again became a focus of public attention when architect Egotov was commissioned to build new

pavilions. Once completed, they became the venue for Russian society to gather during the summer months for music festivals. This brief season of popularity, however, was short-lived. By 1860, Zaryzino was on the point of falling into complete disuse. Plans were made to tear down the entire complex, but they were eventually withdrawn.

From ruin to museum

The first major turning point came after World War II when the Soviets revived Catherine's dream. They set about restoring the architectural monuments and establishing a museum.

Today the park has been restored. The entire area now has an extremely well-tended and inviting appearance. Even on public holidays, countless workers can be seen keeping the paths and grassy areas clean. Such commitment is not accidental—the museum here is dedicated to historic landscape architecture.

For the majority of Muscovites, Zaryzino is a popular destination in both winter and summer, but it is generally visited only by local people, as the park, palace and museum are very rarely mentioned in any up-to-date travel guide.

A picturesque bridge marks the entrance to the palace grounds. The path from the park into the pseudo-Gothic complex leads underneath the archway (top).

The heavily ornate style of the new palace did not meet with Catherine the Great's approval (left).

71

Little Versailles

The Kuskovo Estate outside the gates of Moscow was once the premier venue for sumptuous social occasions

LOCATION:
Yunosti Uliza 2, approximately 7 miles (12km) east of the city center

OPENING TIMES:
10 a.m.–6.m.
(April–October), Closed Mon and Tuesday

GETTING THERE:
Metro: Ryasanskiy Prospect, then Bus: 133 or 208

When the well-to-do Sheremetyev family commissioned a new manor house in the eastern district of Moscow in the mid-18th century, all they really had in mind was a summer residence. When the building work was completed, however, the Russian public were somewhat taken aback—despite the fact that it was just a wooden building on a stone base, Kuskovo, as the country estate was known, had a touch of Versailles about it. Like its royal counterpart in France, this building, constructed in the neoclassical style, radiated a considerable measure of elegance and luxury.

Room for 25,000 guests

Kuskovo still retains much of its fascinating charm to this day: ionic pillars decorate the main façade and portico. This palace-style building was once the venue for the most fashionable parties among Moscow's elite society.

The majestically imposing appearance of the entrance hall contrasts with the surprisingly festive décor of the palace's White Ballroom. Count Sheremetyev, who was then one of the richest men in Russia, could entertain around 25,000 guests at the biggest events. For these occasions, his Grace also maintained his own troupe of actors and musicians on the estate, who had been assembled from his own serfs.

The building's architects designed each room on a different theme. They made generous use of stucco work, pillars, Flemish Gobelin tapestries, English furniture, as well as sculptures and paintings, in order to furnish the rooms and chambers with as much atmosphere as possible.

Popular park

Kuskovo Park, among the biggest and best landscaped gardens in and around the capital, is characterized by the symmetry and uniformity of its dimensions. Strolling along paths lined with sculptures, visitors pass by artificial water features, the Dutch House, which contains a ceramics museum, and arrive finally at the Hermitage.

An Italian grotto was created by the Italian pond and the façade of the Orangery comes into view at the end of the main avenue. Nowadays this is home to the Kuskovo Porcelain Museum and its outstanding collection.

The main manor house is picturesquely situated on the shores of a small lake (above).

Anyone who was permitted to ride up the driveway to the Sheremetyev's family home was a member of Moscow's elite society (far left).

The Orangery now houses a porcelain museum (left).

A country estate outside Moscow

Arkhangelskoye is one of the most delightful pleasure palaces in the vicinity of the capital

Arkhangelskoye is undoubtedly one of the most beautiful noble palaces to be found on the outskirts of Moscow. Its extensive parkland and classical-style, opulently furnished palatial buildings make it one of the most popular destinations for stressed city dwellers, providing a place where they can enjoy gentle walks in the fresh air. A short muse-um visit can also be included, if so desired, as the palace boasts its own art collection.

From palace to sanatorium

Although the general palace complex has been officially closed to visitors for a long time, there was always an opportunity to sneak a glimpse of this wonderful ensemble. A sanatorium for members of the military was set up in the estate's large park during the 1930s, though only for prominent patients. Nevertheless, locals still managed to access the extensive park-land without difficulty—through a hole in the fence.

Some of the most famous names in Russian history are linked with Arkhangelskoye. Its first recorded

LOCATION:
Approximately 15 miles (25 km) west of Moscow, near Krasnogorsk

OPENING TIMES:
10 a.m.–5 p.m., Closed Mon and Tues

GETTING THERE:
Metro: Tushinskaya, then by bus: 549 or Marshrutka: 151

owners were the Princes Odoyevskiy, who were then succeeded by the Golitsyn family. Both these noble families held top positions under the Tsars.

The estate was taken over by Prince Yusopov at the beginning of the 19th century. He is remembered in history as a famous patron of the arts and his extensive collection of paintings can now be viewed in the Pushkin Museum. He is also responsible for the estate's present-day appearance.

Named after the Archangel

Arkhangelskoye—which is the Russian name for Archangel—has a large palace dating from the 18th century. Additional smaller buildings were added, designed by Italian, French and Russian architects.

These include a small tea-house, a pavilion known as "Kaprise," a 17th-century church and another chapel in which the Yusopovs have their final resting-place. All of these are well hidden in a park, the artificially created terraces of which drop gently down toward the Moskva river. The palace view of the river banks is sadly a thing of the past, however. Even so, the park offers a wide range of walks suitable for all seasons.

Past glories

Deliberately neglected during the Soviet era, the buildings have now fallen into a pitiably dilapidated state. The frescoes are gradually peeling off the walls and it is wise to keep well away from the balustrades, which are in a desperate state of repair, while grass grows out of cracks in the palace stonework. The whole complex now belongs to the Russian Ministry of Culture and the progress of the restoration work is very slow.

Unfortunately, only parts of the extensive art collection, which includes paintings, sculptures, porcelain and a library, are open to the public.

With its palace, surrounding buildings, churches and delightful landscaped gardens, Arkhangelskoye is an oasis outside Moscow.

Flourishing landscapes

Thanks to its art and architectural treasures, the Golden Ring is among Europe's greatest cultural landscapes

LOCATION:
North and northeast of Moscow

BEST TIME TO VISIT:
During the summer

GETTING THERE:
By train, bus or car from Moscow

Because the most significant art and cultural centers of Old Russia are arranged in a semicircular pattern around the north and northeast of Moscow, this cultural landscape is known as the "Golden Ring." It encompasses several Old Russian towns, which were closely connected with each other during the Middle Ages both historically and culturally.

On the one hand, this name is an allusion to the golden onion-shaped domes of the churches in these towns. At the same time, however, it is a reference to the gentle central Russian countryside, in which these pearls of urban architecture nestle so harmoniously.

Tourist infrastructure

The towns of the Golden Ring are some of the most visited travel destinations in Russia. Compared with other places, their tourist infrastructure is undeniably well developed. Even during the Communist era, for-

eigners—admittedly only on official tours—were able to visit individual sites along the Golden Ring.

This cultural route could not, however, be admired in its entirety under Soviet rule. Ivanovo, situated half way between Suzdal and Kostroma, was a forbidden city from which foreigners were barred right up until the final days of the Soviet Union.

Art and culture in the provinces

Nowadays, the art and cultural treasures in these cities along the Golden Ring, which survived not only Tatar attacks in the late Middle Ages, but more recent wars as well, can be visited in their entirety. In doing so, it becomes evident just how many remarkable examples of Russian culture and Russian life have flourished here—far away from Moscow and St Petersburg.

Built between the 9th and 11th centuries as northwestern outposts of the mighty Kievan Rus, all the towns on the Golden Ring were constructed around a central fortification system, called a kremlin. Central Russia's natural resources and their location along important trade routes meant that the towns, which had comparatively large populations for medieval times, inevitably grew rapidly.

A flurry of building activity

After the downfall of the Kievan Rus, the territory split up into a large number of independent principalities. Individual rulers competed to make their own capital city into the most sumptuous in the land, which resulted in a large number of superb buildings being erected around this time.

It was important to simultaneously create fortifications and princely residences. As a result, new monasteries, cathedrals and churches have given the towns of Vladimir, Suzdal, Yaroslavl, Rostov-Velikiy, Kostroma, Sergiyev Posad and Pereslavl-Zalesskiy unmistakeable identities, which continue to fascinate visitors to this day.

Invasion by the Tartar armies in 1237-1238 brought an abrupt end to this period of exceptional prosperity and a period of stagnation descended upon the entire region. Moscow, which, up until this time, had been a town of relatively little significance, began to assume a leading role in the struggle against the invaders. From the end of the 14th century, Moscow, now the capital city, outstripped all the others, which gradually declined into provincialism. A large number of art treasures still remain, however, to

bear witness to this period of prosperity. For this reason, UNESCO has designated the old towns along the Golden Ring, as well as individual monuments, as World Cultural Heritage sites.

Perfectly renovated monasteries

Nowhere else in Russia will you find such well-preserved monasteries, palaces and secular buildings. These architectural masterpieces are a powerful indication of the ideals of Old Russia. These towns have not, however, been turned into museum sites.

Many monasteries, which were commandeered or left to fall into ruin during the Soviet period, have since been immaculately restored. Returned into church hands, they now serve once again as sanctuaries for monks. They do, however, remain open to visitors.

The landscape and man's cultural achievements form an inseparable whole along the Golden Ring (above).

The Church of Christ's Transfiguration in Pereslavl was once the burial place of princes (opposite).

View of the Trinity Monastery in Sergiyev Posad, Russia's most important monastery (left).

The soul of Orthodoxy

SERGIYEV POSAD, Russia's most important monastery, is a remarkable architectural ensemble

Sergiyev Posad
Moscow
Russia

LOCATION:
43 miles (70 km) northeast of Moscow; Moscow oblast

SIZE:
Approximately 120,000 inhabitants

GETTING THERE FROM MOSCOW:
Local train: from Yaroslavl Station to Sergiyev Posad or Alexandrov, journey time about 1½ hours

By car: via the Yaroslavskoye Schosse, journey time about 1 hour

Russia's most important monastery is the spiritual center that unites the whole nation. As a symbol of the Russian people's determination to stand their ground, the Trinity Monastery of St Sergius of Radonezh has always bridged the gap between atheists and believers. Its abbots have, for centuries, actively encouraged unity between individual Russian territories under Moscow's leadership.

The combination of traditional Russian architecture and Western influence reflected in the churches and palaces of Sergiyev Posad, Russia's most important monastery complex, had a decisive influence on buildings throughout large parts of Russia. The monastery, with the exception of its museum, was returned to the church in 1991.

Distaste for his contemporaries' preoccupation with lavish architecture drove Sergius, a prince's son, who reputedly lived from 1313 to 1391, to seek refuge from the world. In the mid-14th century he adopted the life of a hermit and retreated to the forests around Radonezh where he erected a simple wooden church. His solitary retreat grew into a monastic community with kitchens, refectory, bakery and two new churches.

Appointed Abbot of the Trinity Monastery by the Metropolitan of Moscow, Sergius became the role model for the perfect monk, committed to converting the people of the North by missionary work. He soon assumed the role of the church's undisputed leading ideologist.

Sergius as the true victor

Sergius, the abbot, however, refused the proffered post as successor to the late Metropolitan and chose instead to retreat from the world in order to immerse himself in religious contemplation. After Grand Prince Dimitriy Donskoy had vanquished what was regarded as the invincible army of the Golden Horde in 1380, his contemporaries regarded Sergius as the true victor.

"God is dead" decreed the Bolsheviks after the October Revolution in 1917. Three years later, they disbanded Russia's most traditional monastery and expelled all the monks and seminarians attending the old Tsarist regime's most venerable theological academy out of the fortified monastery on the eastern outskirts of Sergiyev Posad. Many of its art treasures were brought to Moscow.

Summoning strength for the battle

Sergiyev Posad was renamed *Zagorsk* in 1930 in memory of murdered Party Secretary Vladimir Zagorskiy. However, even the Communists proved unable to eradicate the memory of the canonized founder of the monastery, Sergius of Radonezh, and when Hitler's army invaded the Soviet Union in 1941, Stalin found himself more than ever in need of the support of the Orthodox Church. Believers and atheists alike gathered together in their hour of greatest need before the saint's tomb within the walls of the Trinity Monastery to pray for strength to defend the besieged rodina, or homeland.

Zagorsk was given its old name back in 1991 and the four- to five-hour services that form part of the Orthodox rites have long since resumed in the dimly lit Trinity Cathedral. For many Russians, the extensive monastery citadel crowning Sergiyev Posad has once again become a symbol of their determination to stand their ground in difficult times.

When the Tsars were visiting Sergiyev Posad, they stayed in their own palace (opposite, top left).

The monastery is surrounded by a defense wall, which includes the Carpenter Tower (opposite, top right).

The many different churches, for example, the Chapel by the Well, are richly decorated down to the finest detail (opposite, bottom).

The Church of Our Lady of Smolensk is one of the main churches within the monastery fortress (above).

Trinity Cathedral

No other place is as venerated by the faithful as the tomb of St Sergius, in **SERGIYEV POSAD**

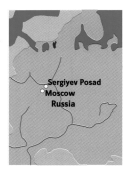

Trinity Cathedral contains the greatest relic of the Russian-Orthodox Church: the tomb of St Sergius (far right).

The Church of the Holy Ghost was designed by Pskov architects (right).

The entrance to the monastery is via the Holy Gateway with its adjacent Gateway Church, which contains numerous frescoes (below).

There must be very few places in the world as richly endowed with churches as the monastery of Sergiyev Posad. In winter especially, when the sun stands high in the vivid blue sky and buildings are dusted with snow, the combined splendor of the dozen churches alone is positively stunning. Yet even though they may indeed vie in beauty with one another, as far as Russian Orthodox Christians are concerned, the undisputed queen of them all is the Trinity Cathedral.

Prayer requests to the Saint

It is here that the grave of Sergius, the founder of the monastery and ideologist, is situated. Continuous streams of people file into the church heading for the silver sarcophagus containing the saint's remains. The faithful patiently await their turn in a long line, which often stretches right back outside the church. Many of the pilgrims leave small slips of paper on the tomb requesting his intercession in having their prayers answered.

For those unfamiliar with the Cathedral's significance, this oldest of the churches within the monastery compound is relatively inconspicuous. This single-domed, four-pillared building with its narrow windows lies somewhat apart from the center of the monastery. Despite its fairly modest dimensions, the church has a distinctly monumental and imposing appearance. The building features just three ornamental friezes, which soften the somewhat severe overall appearance of the façades. The church was designed in the 15th century, since which time this white limestone Trinity Cathedral has overshadowed all other churches in the country.

Church of the Holy Ghost

The Church of the Holy Ghost, on the other hand, lies directly in front of the visitors as they step inside the monastery walls. It was the work of architects from Pskov. The building, completed in 1476, consists of a church topped with a bell-tower, designed in the old style as a single structure.

In keeping with the architectural traditions of this northern Russian town, the architects' design for the building incorporated massive cylindrical pillars on which rest the entire weight of the domed belfry.

This small church is a slender, square structure and considerably more graceful in appearance than the nearby Trinity Cathedral.

A Stroganov-style gateway church

Access to the monastery complex on its eastern side is through the Holy Gate, where the visitor will encounter the Gateway Church of the Nativity of St John the Baptist. It was constructed in 1692 from funds donated by the affluent Stroganov merchant family.

Frescoes decorating the passageway depict events from the life of the monastery's founder. The iconostasis created by Andrei Rublev and Daniil Chornyi has been preserved in its original splendor. Nearby, the Nikon Chapel, constructed to house the tomb of Abbot Nikon, who succeeded Sergius in office, contrasts elegantly with the Cathedral.

Monastic bells

SERGIYEV POSAD contains the Chapel by the Well, a bell tower, and the Tsar's residence

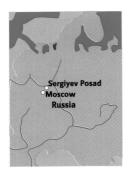

The bell tower, regarded as the most beautiful of its kind in all Russia, soars majestically upward (right).

The well, from which pilgrims extract holy water, is situated in a fairy-tale setting. The Tsar's palace can be seen in the background (far right).

A small chapel has been erected, named the red Chapel by the Well, in honor of the water's curative powers (below).

The faithful flock from all over Russia to this monastery fortress, extensively restored in 1938 when its defense wall, measuring almost 4,593ft (1,400 m), was reconstructed down to the smallest detail. Visitors buy candles and, during the summer months, *kvass*, Russia's national beverage, from the monks. Or, alternatively, they make their way to the Chapel by the Well.

Here there is a constant stream of people filling bottles they have brought along with "St Sergius water," which is famed for its miraculous qualities. It is even claimed to be holy water. The well was discovered in 1644 and a small chapel was built over it. Its unusual diversity of form and color automatically make it a major focus of interest.

A model residence for the Tsars

The rooms in the Tsar's residence, which was completed toward the end of the 17th century as a replacement for an earlier wooden building, were fashioned in the Baroque style. The palace, which was situated along the north wall and modeled on the design of the refectory with check patterns and opulently decorated windows, was to serve as a model for subsequent Tsarist residences throughout the land. A particularly distinctive feature of this architectural monument are the window surrounds on the main floor, where a series of private rooms and staterooms used by the Tsar are situated.

A patriotic manastery

Tsarina Elisaveta Petrovna conferred the title of Lavra (main monastery) on the Trinity Monastery in 1744, thereby giving it equal status with the Monastery of the Kiev Caves, the Pochayevsk Monastery, and the Alexander Nevsky Monastery in St Petersburg. Consequently, the Abbot became the richest landowner in Russia after the Tsar.

Such an increase in power was reflected in architectural terms. Italian architect Bartolomeo Francesco Rastrelli, for example, designed an 288-ft (88-m) high bell tower, intended as a symbol of the monastery's wealth.

The most beautiful bell tower

Legend has it that it tops the bell tower in Moscow's Kremlin by 20ft (6m). This elegant, soaring blue-white tower, the four levels of which rest on a square plinth, is said to be Russia's most beautiful bell tower.

Onion domes

The Cathedral of the Assumption in **SERGIYEV POSAD** has a distinct appearance

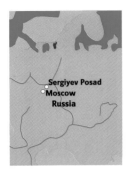

The Cathedral of the Assumption is the largest church within the monastery complex. Its central golden dome is a prominent landmark visible from afar (right).

The church is decorated inside and out with depictions of the Virgin Mary (above right).

Despite its rather austere interior, the atmosphere inside the cathedral is very peaceful (opposite, bottom).

The most distinctive church in the monastery, situated in the very heart of the complex, is the Cathedral of the Assumption. The Dormition Cathedral, as it is also called, not only has a rather somber exterior, but is also fairly restrained on the inside. It consequently contrasts sharply with the bright and cheerful appearance of the nearby Chapel by the Well and the well itself.

Modeled on the Cathedral of the Assumption in the Moscow Kremlin, which was the Tsars' coronation church, this church, the largest in the monastery complex, was built in 1584 by Ivan the Terrible, who commissioned it following his victory over the Tatars.

A few years after the commencement of construction work, however, the Tsar's enthusiasm for the project began to wane as the monastery became increasingly opposed to his oprichnina—Ivan's personal household guard, whom he had settled in quarters close to the monastery.

Sample of the Baroque

This church, the interior of which is famous for its frescoes, is topped by five imposing onion-shaped domes, the central one gleaming gold in the sunlight and the others a vivid blue. Together they form one of the monastery's unmistakable landmarks.

The distinctly austere and rather plain appearance of the exterior is echoed on the inside. The magnificent frescoes, painted around 1648 by Yaroslavl painters, are dominated by blue and violet tones, which give the works a somewhat restrained character. Legend has it that it took the men just 100 days to create these monumental works which are so typical of their school.

Looking at these frescoes, it is easy to see how church painting progressed during this period from idealistic to realistic representation. The richly decorated iconostasis may be viewed as a precursor to the Baroque movement of the 18th century.

Final resting-place of Tsar Boris

Boris Godunov was laid to rest next to his wife and two sons behind the Cathedral of the Assumption. Murdered by an assassin, this ruler was denied burial in the Moscow Kremlin.

A stately monastery

The churches of **SERGIYEV POSAD** are sumptuous and lavish

Sergiyev Posad
Moscow
Russia

The refectory is more like a palace than a church (top right).

The ceilings are decorated with frescoes embellished with gold (top left).

The overall view of the large hall illustrates the enormous wealth that was in the hands of the monastery (bottom right).

The delicate little church of Our Lady of Smolensk was completed in 1753 and is in keeping with the St Petersburg Baroque style. It was built by Alexei Razumovski, the then favorite of Tsarina Elisaveta, daughter of Peter the Great. To create space for the church, the old monastery kitchen dating from the mid-18th century was demolished. Painted blue and white, the church has an octagonal ground plan. Concave and convex sides alternate regularly. One could easily be forgiven for thinking that this seems more like a fanciful retreat in a landscaped garden than a place of devotion and prayer.

Richly decorated dining hall

The refectory was similarly commissioned by Ivan IV—its lavish decoration was not at all in keeping with the simple lifestyle of the monks. The dining hall, which measures 5490ft^2 (510m^2), features distinctive diamond-patterned exterior walls and pillars, entwined with stone carvings of vines. Baroque stucco work, ceiling and wall frescoes decorate the ceremonial hall of the refectory and the extravagant splendor continues on the outside with a façade decorated in a geometric pattern of green, blue, yellow and red. The wide cornice rests on half-pillars creating an open gallery and a series of arches, decorated with shells, to form a coronet around the upper edge of the classical-style attic.

Impressions from the past

The sight of visitors strolling along the paths, deep in heart-to-heart conversations with the monks, is one which could easily lead the observer to feel he had slipped back in time to prerevolutionary Russia. This peaceful scene, however, effectively masks the fact that the monastery and state have been at odds with each other for years.

Moscow refuses to return several original Rublev icons, which were brought to the Tretyakov Gallery after the monastery's possessions were seized by the state. Furthermore, the church has, for many years, been demanding that it should have responsibility for running the well-endowed monastery museum within the hospital. The government, however, is determined to keep it under state control.

Old Russia at its best

Virtually no other Russian town is as well preserved as **SUZDAL**

LOCATION:
136 miles (220km)
northeast of Moscow

SIZE:
approximately 12,000
inhabitants

**GETTING THERE FROM
MOSCOW:**
By rail: From Kurski
Station by express train
to Vladimir, journey
time about 2 hours,
then by bus

A visit to the small town of Suzdal
will lead you directly back into
the past of Old Russia. Records show
that it was founded during the 12th
century in the midst of gently rolling
hills and green meadows either side of
the Kamenka river. As the religious
and artistic heart of Old Russia, Suzdal, a town "under God's protection,"
became the center for more architectural monuments than any other
comparable towns in the region, even
the layout of the streets of the prince's
residence have remained unchanged
for centuries.

The mighty square limestone
cathedrals of Suzdal and Vladimir
were constructed during the heyday
of the Vladimir-Suzdal empire. These
gleaming white, beautifully restored
buildings symbolized the princes'
determination to break free from the
Byzantine yoke. No Soviet-style concrete building or factory plant has
been allowed to spoil the appearance

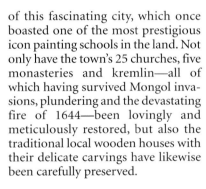

of this fascinating city, which once boasted one of the most prestigious icon painting schools in the land. Not only have the town's 25 churches, five monasteries and kremlin—all of which having survived Mongol invasions, plundering and the devastating fire of 1644—been lovingly and meticulously restored, but also the traditional local wooden houses with their delicate carvings have likewise been carefully preserved.

Eastern outpost

The legendary Prince Yuri Dolgoruky (1125–1157) began by founding Kiev, then went into battle against rival principalities in the region "behind the forests" between the Volga and Oka rivers. It was here that he established the fortified settlement of Suzdal as an outpost on the edge of the vast Asiatic expanses. Suzdal remained the capital city for over three decades. In 1157, however, Vladimir assumed the leading role in the principality of Vladimir-Suzdal.

At the beginning of 1238, both towns fell into the hands of the Mongols, led by Batu Khan, who by 1240 had succeeded in capturing every Russian town except for Novgorod and advanced as far as what is now Poland.

Suzdal's oldest church is the Cathedral of the Nativity of the Virgin, which was built between 1222 and 1256. Its design is modeled on St Sophia's Cathedral in Kiev and based on a Byzantine cross with Roman elements. Since the mid-17th century, the Cathedral has been crowned by five blue star-studded onion-shaped domes. Its golden doors are among the oldest and most impressive examples of cast-iron work.

Using this method, copper plates were covered with black lacquer, followed by a layer of beeswax. After engraving the designs, the master craftsman poured gold amalgam over the plates. While the mercury evaporated, the copper and gold became a firm compound.

Old Russia transfigured

Behind the Kremlin walls resides the Archbishop, in whose palace a museum has been established. The Church of St Nicholas with its flat tent roof and graceful onion-shaped cupola was constructed in 1720. It is particularly noted for the sumptuous framework surrounding its windows and portals.

The wooden Church of St Nicholas, built in 1766—one of seven wooden churches in Suzdal's kremlin—was brought to Suzdal from the village of Glotovo in 1960. For anyone seeking a nostalgic experience, Suzdal is the ideal destination. Many people regard the town's flawlessly preserved appearance as a perfect example of what is now a frequently idealized image of Old Russia.

Fortified monastery citadels

A ring of fortified monasteries was built around **SUZDAL** in order to defend it against attack

LOCATION:
136 miles (220 km)
northeast of Moscow

SIZE:
Approximately 12,000
inhabitants

**GETTING THERE FROM
MOSCOW:**
By rail: From Kurski
Station by express train
to Vladimir, journey
time about 2 hours,

A mighty ring of 15 monasteries outside the town walls once provided Suzdal with additional protection. Some of these are among the great masterpieces of Russian architecture.

Monastery of the Deposition of the Holy Robe

One of the most outstanding architectural complexes is the Monastery of the Deposition of the Holy Robe, built in 1207. In 1688, it acquired the Holy Gate at its entrance. This consists of a base topped with two pyramid-shaped turrets, finished in glazed tiles. The yellow bell tower, visible from afar, is one of the town's best-known landmarks. A viewing terrace is incorporated on the upper level, which provides magnificent panoramic views over Suzdal and the gently rolling landscape.

Alexander Nevsky himself donated the Alexandrovsky Convent in the northwestern district of the town. It still retains enough of its former splendor to illustrate just how magnificent the building once was. Only the Church of Christ's Ascension, the Holy Gate and the bell tower, however, have withstood the ravages of time.

Savior Monastery of St Euthymius

Behind a high defense wall, fortified by a dozen mighty round towers, is Suzdal's most famous monastery, the splendidly ornate Savior Monastery of St. Euthymius.

It contains Russia's oldest tent-roofed church, the Assumption Refectory Church, constructed in 1525. Its main gate, completed in 1664, is a massive rectangular structure, 72ft (22 m) in height and topped by a domed tent roof.

No less impressive is the Church of the Annunciation, which had a predominantly defensive role. In 1990, the old bells of varying sizes were rehung in the bell tower of the Cathedral of the Transfiguration.

For seven decades, the church had been strictly prohibited from calling the faithful to prayer by ringing the

The white monastery buildings of Suzdal delight the visitor who sets out on a voyage of discovery to explore this magical landscape. The wonderful chimes ring out far across the countryside from Suzdal's famous bell tower.

bells. After the October Revolution, any bells regarded as insignificant in terms of art history were simply melted down without further ado. Only composers and music researchers were allowed to have anything to do with them and then purely in scientific terms.

The Russians and their bells

Since the fall of Communism, music students can once again study the art of bell-ringing, an art form which had virtually died out. For the monastery chimes to ring out as melodiously as they did in the days of Old Russia, it requires three or four bell-ringers to work together in unison.

Despite the seventy-year ban, virtually no other nation is as intimately attached to its bells, which were first introduced by the Byzantine masters, as the Russian people are. In contrast to the practice in West European countries, it is not the bell that is swung back and forth in Russia, but the clapper.

A monastery hotel

The Cathedral of Pokrovsky Monastery can be seen from afar. It was formerly an Intourist Hotel for foreigners and VIPs. For this reason, the historic building was better preserved than other monasteries. Nuns have now resumed residence here once more.

Byzantine models

The sumptuous churches of **VLADIMIR** equaled the churches of Constantinople and Kiev in every respect

LOCATION:
118 miles (190km) northeast of Moscow

SIZE:
Approximately 400,000 inhabitants

GETTING THERE FROM MOSCOW:
By rail: from Kurski Station by express train; journey time about 2 hours

By car: via Highway M7, journey time about 2½ hours

Intended originally as a medieval fortress, Vladimir has quickly grown into an industrial town since the beginning of the last century. Very little is left now to remind us of the charm of Old Russia. What does remain, however, is well worth a visit. This includes the cathedral, the palace of Prince Andrey Bogolyubsky, and the Golden Gate, all of which now lie isolated in the midst of a busy city.

The new capital
At the beginning of the 12th century, Prince Vladimir II Monomakh had a fortress built on the banks of the Klyasma river, a tributary of the Volga, and gave the place his own name. Just half a century later, Vladimir became the new capital of the principality of Rostov-Suzdal.

A visitor to the town would enter through the Golden Gate, which owes its name to its gilded copper finish. Behind this was situated the inner citadel with the prince's palace, churches and bishop's residence, modeled on Byzantium and Kiev. The most famous architectural monuments of Kiev and Constantinople were models for the design of the

Cathedral of the Assumption, begun in 1158. Its carved reliefs and decorative wall friezes were the work of stonemasons from Lombardy.

The Cathedral, constructed from huge blocks of limestone, was intended to symbolize the express will of the ruler of the principality of Vladimir-Suzdal to break free from domination by the Byzantine church. Even today, the impression still lingers that this mighty church is hovering between heaven and earth.

Pyramidal dome structure
In their design of Vladimir's massive Cathedral of the Assumption, which, until the Metropolitan seat was moved to Moscow in 1326, was the mother church of all Russia, the architects repeated the pyramidal dome construction, which gives the St Sophia Cathedral in Kiev its unmistakable profile.

Its design features a series of round arches. The areas between the small pillars of the arcature once contained paintings of high priests and prophets. The interior boasts well preserved frescoes by the two icon painters Andrei Rublyev and Daniil Chorny (1408).

Church of St Demetrius
Toward the end of the 12th century, the princes commissioned a royal chapel dedicated to St Demetrius to be built as a counterpart to the highly prominent cathedral on the steep slope leading down to the River Klyazma.

Roman influence is evident in the design of this church, constructed in the shape of a cross with a single dome. It is elaborately decorated with numerous relief images of well over 1,000 sculptures depicting mythical figures and legendary creatures. The sculptural décor remains a source of fascination even today: it is supposed to symbolize the powerful and united princedom of God's grace. Anyone wanting to view the town's most famous artwork, however, will have to travel to Moscow.

The "Our Lady of Vladimir" icon, which marked the beginning of Russian icon painting, was only restored in 1918 after being rediscovered near the Tsar's Gate. The image was revealed after being concealed beneath later layers of paint. Shortly afterward, the "Vladimirskaya" was transferred to the Tretyakov Gallery.

The numerous towers of Vladimir's churches soar majestically heav-enward (above and opposite).

The "Golden Gates," constructed in the 12th century, are a rare example of Old Russian military construction, comprising a 45-ft (14-m) high tower topped with a church. This magnificent piece of architecture is the last of five such impressive structures (left).

Symphony in stone

Older than Moscow, the cultural center of **ROSTOV VELIKI** developed its own style of architecture in the 17th century

LOCATION:
approximately 125 miles (200km) from Moscow; Yaroslavl oblast

SIZE:
about 34,000 inhabitants

GETTING THERE FROM MOSCOW:
By rail: from Yaroslavl Station, journey time about 3 hours

Along the unfortified shore of Lake Nero, well-trodden trails lead past rolling hills and wooden houses into the old part of the town, where cathedrals and palaces tower above the walls of the picturesque kremlin. According to the *Chronicle of Nestor*, one of the oldest Russian historical accounts, Rostov was founded by Rurik the Varangian in 862 as one of the capital cities of the Old Russian Empire. This makes Rostov almost three centuries older than Moscow.

Rostov the Great
Trade and commerce flourished to such an extent that in the 13th centu-

ry, this thriving center began to call itself, quite unabashedly, Rostov Veliki, or Rostov the Great. Among the most important items produced by local craftsmen were enamel paintings, created primarily by monks affiliated to the Rostov-Suzdal school of icon painting in their monastery workshops and Rostov *finift*, as enamel is called in Russian, was much prized at royal courts all over the empire.

From the very beginning, Rostov played a leading role in resisting Tatar rule. The first uprising against these heathen masters from the steppes took place in 1262. Sergius of Radonezh, a leading 14th-century

theologian and statesman, hailed from a Rostov monastery from where, by dint of rhetoric, he orchestrated the first revival of the Old Russian Empire.

Ornate wooden houses
Despite the fact that it was fashionable in the 17th century for Russian towns to be redesigned in the Naryshkin Baroque style, Rostov's architects went their own way and developed an individual style based on traditional church architecture as it had been before the Mongol invasion. During the century that followed, Catherine II had Rostov large-

The Monastery of St. Jacob was occupied by simple peasant families from the surrounding area after the complex was desecrated by the new rulers after the October Revolution

ly rebuilt according to a systematic ground-plan.

Classicism was the next movement to influence this lakeside city. Natural stone or brick was used for important buildings although living quarters continued to be constructed mainly of wood and decorated with painted carvings. Even nobles, merchants and industrialists had wooden residences.

Contemporary writers waxed lyrical about Rostov in the 19th century, describing it as a "symphony in stone." The more recent ring road with its representational public buildings encircles a broad belt of parks and gardens, which surround the center with its marketplace and five-domed Savior Church.

A patriarch in the kremlin

The heart of the town is dominated by the kremlin with its architectural monuments and art treasures. Secular princes have never resided here— it has instead always served as the Patriarch's residence, symbolizing the church's superiority over worldly powers.

Rostov's most imposing church is the Cathedral of the Assumption, built in the 16th century, which is crowned by five mighty onion-shaped domes. Next to the church is Rostov's famous set of bells—it is said that these could once be heard up to 12 miles (20km) away.

Opposite the cathedral, the route leads through a gate into the interior of the kremlin to the Church of the Resurrection, framed by two round towers. The Metropolitan's court was, after all, formerly the Patriarch's residence, parts of which now serve as a museum. Rostov's most important monasteries include the Yakovlev Monastery of Our Savior on the shores of Lake Nero and the Abraham Monastery with the Epiphany Cathedral completed in 1553.

The October Revolution signaled Rostov's decline. The new regime's first steps included banning any ringing of the bells and driving the monks from the monasteries.

Peasant families from the surrounding countryside took up residence in the monks' cells of the Monastery of St. Jacob and the monastery that produced Sergius of Radonezh was turned into a poultry farm. Two other monasteries were disbanded and less than half of the original 20 churches survived.

A sinking city

For many years, a serious geological problem has been causing a great deal of concern to conservationists: these cultural monuments were built on marshy ground and are slowly sinking. The European Council in Strasbourg has now begun to address the problem posed by this town on Lake Nero. The primary task is to stabilize the ground beneath the structures before restoring the historic buildings.

Culture behind the woods

PERESLAVL-ZALESSKY was once an important center of trade with Western Europe. The famous hilltop monastery originates from this period

LOCATION:
On Lake Pleshcheyevo, 80 miles (130km) north-east of Moscow; Yaroslavl oblast

SIZE:
Approximately 43,000 inhabitants

GETTING THERE FROM MOSCOW:
Local train: from Yaroslavl Station towards Sergiyev Posad, then by bus, journey time about 3 hours

Dark forests dominated the land-scape around Pereslavl in the Middle Ages which is why the town, founded by Yuri Dolgoruky in 1152, also became known as *Zalessky*, "behind the woods." The most important historic architectural ensemble here is the once prosperous hilltop monastery.

Situated on a trade route

Despite its name, this thriving town was never a backwoods. Pereslavl reached the peak of its prosperity as a center of commerce during the 12th century owing to its situation on an important route linking Moscow with Archangelsk in the far north. Trade flourished accordingly.

Its good fortune did not last, how-ever—Tatar armies overran Pereslavl on a number of occasions and virtu-ally razed it to the ground. Neverthe-less, the inhabitants did not lose heart and simply rebuilt their town on each occasion.

A new phase in Pereslavl's devel-opment began when it became part of Muscovy in 1302. It was around this time in the early 14th century that the famous monastery was founded. It grew in importance as the monks received numerous gifts in the form of villages, mills and saltworks. The 16th century heralded a major phase in its economic growth during which Pereslavl even entered into close trade relations with partners in several Western-European countries.

In the style of St Petersburg Baroque

Pereslavl's fortified mountain monas-tery is accessed through the Holy Gate, above which rises the Church of St Nicholas with its fine stucco work in the Moscow style. The Cathedral of the Assumption, the most important of the monastery's churches, was built later in 1757 and decorated in the St. Petersburg Baroque style.

Trinity Cathedral, the interior of which was decorated with frescoes during the 17th century, was con-structed in 1530 in the Trinity Danilov Monastery and is solemnly austere in appearance. The only sur-viving part of this former monastery enclosure is the Gate of Honor.

Elegant dining hall

Nothing of the kremlin building itself has survived—save for its churches. Two of the finest include the Cathe-dral of the Transfiguration of the Sav-ior, founded in 1152, and the tent-roofed Church of Peter the Metro-politan. The Niketas Monastery, finally, boasts the Niketas Cathedral, a 16th-century cross-shaped struc-ture, topped by five cupolas. The refectory, redesigned in Moscow Baroque style, will fascinate the visi-tor with its elegant proportions.

This once-imposing mountain monastery received numerous gifts in the form of villages, mills and saltworks. It quickly developed into an important center of commerce and has remained so to this day.

97

Classic elegance

The city's palaces and Russia's most beautiful Baroque church reflect **KOSTROMA'S** golden age

LOCATION:
230 miles (372km) northeast of Moscow

SIZE:
approximately 280,000 inhabitants

GETTING THERE FROM MOSCOW:
By rail: from Yaroslavl Station, journey time about 7 hours;

By bus: journey time about 8 hours

By car: via the Yaroslavskoye Schosse, journey time about 4½ hours

Long ago, great cathedrals dominated the skyline of this old trading town on the upper reaches of the Volga, lending it an unmistakable profile. Approaching Kostroma today, however, one's gaze is drawn inexorably to the huge concrete giants of the 1930s. It was Kostroma, of all places, a town that owed its prosperity to the manufacture of sailcloth, that the Soviet leaders singled out for their grandiose modernization projects.

Despite the impairment of its historic image, Kostroma, even today, remains a fascinating destination on account of its superb examples of ecclesiastical architecture. The Church of the Resurrection in the Grove, which dates from the 17th century, is by far the most outstanding architectural group in this part of the country.

A monastery as a cultural center

Once a thriving center of crafts and trade, Kostroma, the first recorded mention of which was in 1213, became part of the principality of Moscow in the 16th century. At this time, the famous Hypatian Monastery of Kostroma was developing into one of the most influential cultural centers in Russia. The bulky-looking Voskoboynaya Tower, which forms part of the monastery's defense fortifications, survives from this time.

The Tsars were constantly altering Kostroma's appearance. One of the most dramatic changes took place in 1642: during just three years of construction, Moscow's rulers reshaped the town southwest of the monastery to conform to a rectangular groundplan. In 1955, the Church of the Transfiguration of Christ, originally situated in a neighboring village, was moved here. This wooden church which was built on wooden piles consists of a single room.

Old Russian wooden architecture

Kostroma's architectural centerpiece with its five golden domes is the Trinity Cathedral, which was built in 1588. It features several porches, each with a tent roof, as a well as a gallery running around it. Outstanding

examples of the art of wooden architecture, including churches, houses, and other types of wooden structures, are now on public display in an open-air museum.

During the reign of Catherine the Great, a large number of classical-style buildings were constructed in the historic heart of Kostroma. The layout was based on a fan-shaped design. Many medieval buildings have also survived. The trading rows, as the market arcades are known, were extremely important in their day and include the flour rows, which were completed in the late 18th century.

Neoclassical ensemble

Opposite these are the "Beautiful Rows" which, together with the Fire Watch Tower, form the main elements of a remarkable neoclassical grouping—guardhouse, General Borshchov's House and a public adminis-

The wintry landscape gives the pleasure gardens with their rotundas a magical appearance (right).

Pile dwellings are a common sight bordering the region's riverbanks (center).

The famous trading arcades, built in the 18th century by Catherine the Great, with their classical-style bell tower (top right).

The imperial yellow fire tower in Kostroma city center (bottom right).

trative building, together with other commercial buildings, complete the southern side of the square.

The Church of the Resurrection in the Grove, the most important church on the Volga, is noted for its superb façade—half-pillars arranged in pairs, a gallery of arches and three-side staircase structures topped with tiled roofs combine to create a harmonious whole. The carved reliefs depict pelicans, unicorns and lions, themes that contribute to this church's magical appearance.

Magnificently decorated on the outside, the church will captivate the visitor on the inside with its exquisite treasures. The walls are lavishly covered with frescoes portraying scenes from the Apocalypse and the story of Adam and Eve.

Memories of Jerusalem

The Resurrection Monastery near Istra is the only sacred building
in Russia to have architectural associations with Jerusalem

Because the landscape around the new monastery near Istra, not far from Moscow, had similarities with the area around Jerusalem, it was named "New Jerusalem."

For much of its length, the little Istra River flows past fields and wooded meadows until it abruptly changes direction. Crowning the hilltop on this bend in the river is one of Old Russia's most legendary monasteries: the monastery of Novo Jerussalim, or New Jerusalem.

It was founded in 1657 by the powerful Patriarch Nikon, who originally intended the monastery as a country seat. During the protracted planning phase, while the site was vis-ited by Tsar Alexey Mikhailovich and his retinue, a theologian, who happened to be present and who had visited the Holy Land, remarked that the surrounding landscape reminded him very much of Jerusalem. Tsar Alexey was so taken with this comparison that he expressed the wish that the monastery be named after the Holy City.

Enthusiastic involvement

Nikon, who renounced his position as Patriarch in 1658, became very much involved in the monastery's construction. He was extremely assiduous about supervising the individual building phases of the cathedral, the design of which was based on the Church of the Holy Sepulchre in Jerusalem.

The very size of the Cathedral of the Resurrection lends it a majestic appearance; its interior is one of the most precious of any monastery in Russia. Shaped in the form of a cross, this sacred building features a great many cornices and window surrounds, which are lavishly decorated with green glazed "peacock's eye" tiles.

Inside the cathedral, a copy of the sepulcher was created at a depth of 20ft (6m) and a large number of icons decorate the interior. Nowadays, the monastery serves as a museum and art gallery.

LOCATION:
35 miles (56km) west of Moscow; Moscow oblast

SIZE:
Approximately 34,000 inhabitants

GETTING THERE FROM MOSCOW:
By rail: toward Riga

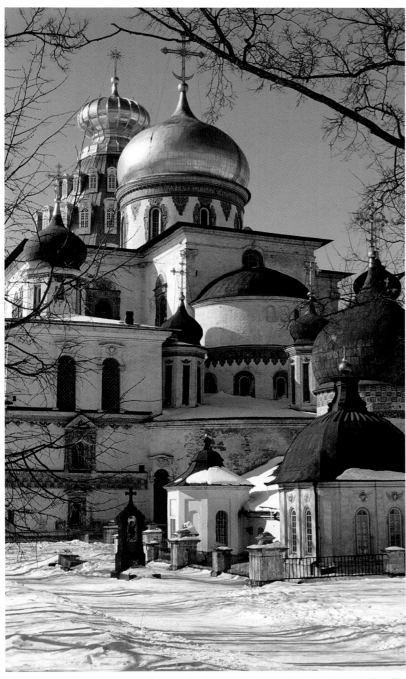

The white walls and towers of the majestic monastery can be seen rising in the distance as one approaches Novo Jerussalim, which is crowned by the golden dome of the Cathedral of the Resurrection.

Risen from the ruins

RYAZAN was once one of the most important towns in Old Russia until it was destroyed by the Tatars. In the 17th century, however, an architectural jewel arose from the ruins

It hardly seems possible now that Ryazan, the central town of the principality of that name, was once one of the most thriving cities in Old Russia. With the exception of one church, nothing survives from that era preceding the Mongol invasion. When Pereslavl-Ryazansky, as it was formerly known, was overrun in 1237 by riders of the Golden Horde, it was completely destroyed.

Fresh beginnings

Over the course of centuries, however, the town gradually recovered although it never fully regained its original importance. It did, however, experience a period of economic boom during the 17th century and it was during this time that the town began to take on the picturesque appearance that greets us today. The design of the newly constructed churches and monasteries clearly reflects the strong influence of Moscow architecture.

The Naryshkin Baroque style was particularly fashionable during this era.

Ryazan's most important church, the Cathedral of the Assumption, alternatively known as the Dormition Cathedral, is situated in the kremlin and was commissioned by Metropolitan Hilarion at the end of the 17th century. Its design incorporated a generous interior, the most valuable treasure of which is a Baroque iconostasis. The construction of the bell tower proved to be a successful combination of several different styles.

Construction of the Cathedral of the Savior's Transfiguration began in the early 18th century. It is particularly famous for its ornately glazed tiles. Next to it is the Archbishop's Palace. Two tent roofs crown the Church of the Holy Ghost, which was completed in 1642.

Classicism

The Cathedral of the Archangel dates back to the 16th century, but has been altered several times right up until the 19th century. It serves as the final resting-place for Ryazan's princes. It contains icons that provide the visitor with an idea of its earlier décor as well as a famous altar cloth.

As the era of classicism gained pace, Ryazan also underwent some marked changes. In 1780, the city was redesigned according to a checkerboard layout. Public buildings continued to be built.

Art Nouveau influence

Toward the end of the 19th century, Fyodor Shekhtel, considered Russia's leading architect of the Art Nouveau School, left his mark on the town when he drafted the design for the Dervis house at Kiritsy.

Just north of Ryazan is another monastery of regional importance. Though founded in the 14th century, buildings in the monastery complex, such as the Holy Ghost Church, date from the 17th century.

LOCATION:
125 miles (200km) southeast of Moscow, Ryazan oblast

SIZE:
Approximately 520,000 inhabitants

The magnificent Uspensky Cathedral is the city's distinctive landmark. It was built between 1693 and 1699 and covers an area of 17,220ft² (1,600m²). Its tower is 236ft (72m) in height and one of its most precious treasures is an enormous 88ft (27m) high iconostasis (top left).

Boggy marsh areas are a typical feature of the region's low-lying landscape (left).

Russia's link to the West

Under Peter the Great, ST PETERSBURG grew from nothing into a new capital

ADDRESS:
Russia, St Petersburg, 191060 Smolny (city administration)

LOCATION:
In the northwest of Russia where the Neva river flows into the Baltic

SIZE:
Approximately 4,600,000 inhabitants

SPECIAL FEATURES:
Renamed "St Petersburg" soon after it was founded, it was renamed "Petrograd" between 1914 and 1924, then became "Leningrad" from 1924 to 1991

In a poetic tribute to St Petersburg, the Russian poet Alexander Pushkin compared the former Tsarist capital with a stern, slender woman. More than 300 years after it was founded, this stony beauty is looking every bit of her age. Despite having kept her fascinating looks, the wrinkles—in the form of buildings off the main streets, desperately in need of restoration—are very much in evidence.

A Tsar's determination

Anyone visiting this city will find it hard to believe that it represents the vision—turned into reality—of just one man, Peter the Great. The Tsar wanted to equip his empire with a gateway to the West, ideally via the sea—and in his view, Moscow was completely unsuitable in this respect. He consequently broke with all tradition and decided to build a new capital city, siting it at the point where the Neva flows into the Baltic Sea.

Tsar Peter's surprising decision to transfer his government to the inhospitable North initially caused horror among his court officials. Never in their wildest dreams had they imagined exchanging their beautiful city of Moscow for a primitive pioneer settlement—and one that was uncomfortably close to Sweden, an as yet unvanquished enemy. However, after the 1709 victory over Sweden at Poltava, Russian court officials were left with no choice but to pack their bags and move north. The systematic development of the Tsar's new seat of government, which—apart from a brief interlude—remained the country's capital city from 1712 to 1918, represents what is without doubt the most amazing feat of urban development of the entire 18th century, for St Petersburg was, right from the start, envisaged as a major city with various commercial centers.

Superhuman feat

In human terms, of course, this feat of achievement represents an unprecedented brutality. Tens of thousands of Swedish and Turkish prisoners-of-war were forced to toil for years erecting buildings in this hostile territory, incurring heavy losses in the process. In order to stabilize the frequently flooded ground, they drove countless tree trunks into the mud.

Working to a largely systematic ground-plan designed by French architect Alexandre Leblond, the forced laborers built a city which spanned 42 islands as well as 65 Neva tributaries and canals—a city with dimensions which were extraordinary for that period.

The huge monumentality of the architecture in *Pitersburch* as the Tsar called "Russia's window to the West," was in itself a clear indication of the Tsar's ambition to assume a leading role among the major powers of 18th-century Europe in both the political and cultural spheres.

St Petersburg which, thanks to the skills of the most famous architects from Italy, France and Germany, was destined to become Europe's most beautiful city, was conceived as a complete opposite to traditional Moscow, a city which had turned its back on Europe and which the Tsar scornfully referred to as a "large village."

When Moscow was rebuilt after the fires of 1812, St Petersburg, with its Baroque Classical-style architecture, was used as a model. Its long, Parisian-style boulevards, wide squares and large expanses of green park were also copied by towns in the south of Russia, such as Odessa and Sevastapol.

At the heart of the new settlement, Peter, a restless spirit who throughout his life also demonstrated considerable talent as a craftsman, ordered the building of the Peter and Paul Fortress and a shipyard. The first, fairly modest stone buildings were the work of the Ticino architect, Domenico Trezzini, who also produced the designs for the rows of wooden houses, the Twelve Colleges, as the individual ministries were known, as well as the first of the landscaped parks.

The city's design has been respected by all subsequent rulers—even the Soviets left it untouched.

ST PETERSBURG

Even the Soviets respected the uniformity of the historic old town and no modern high-rise building has been allowed to spoil the view (above).

The red Rostra Columns once guided ships into St Petersburg harbor. In the background is the yellow tower of the Cathedral of Peter and Paul (left).

Birthplace of the city

The Peter and Paul Fortress is the original heart of St Petersburg. This imposing building is now an impressive attraction

ADDRESS:
Petropavlovskaya
Krepost

OPENING TIME:
Daily 11 a.m.-5 p.m.,
Tues 11 a.m.-4 p.m.,
closed Wed and the last
Tues of the month; the
fortress itself can be
accessed daily up until
10 p.m.

GETTING THERE:
Metro: Gorkovksaya;
Bus: 46; Tram: 2, 40

Every day at noon, a loud boom can be heard on the outskirts of the city. This daily event, which tourists tend to find rather disconcerting when they first hear it, has been a traditional part of life for the citizens for a very long time. It is a reminder of St Petersburg's oldest building, the Peter and Paul Fortress, which forms the nucleus of the city.

The firing of the cannon at the Naryshkin Bastion has been a tradition since the 18th century, almost since this imposing fortification was first established on Hare Island in the middle of the Neva delta.

The first cornerstone was laid on May 16, 1703—around 20,000 men worked on the building, which was designed by Peter the Great and intended as a bastion against the Swedes in the Great Northern War (1700–1721). The construction initially consisted of timber defense walls, which were quickly replaced in 1706 with an encircling stone wall, measuring 8–14ft (2.5–4 m) thick, in the shape of an irregular hexagon.

From fortress to prison

Architect Domenico Trezzini directed this vast building project, which covered the whole of Hare Island, an area of 2,296 x 1,312ft (700x400m).

Adjacent to the defense wall, the laborers constructed various bastions, named after the ruler and his contemporaries Naryshkin, Trubezkoy, Sotov, Golovkin and Menshikov. Additional protection was provided in the form of several defense outworks, known as ravelins.

The Peter and Paul Fortress, with all its fortifications enclosed within its ramparts, was completed in the middle of the 18th century. All this construction work proved unnecessary, however, since the building was never required for defensive purposes. From 1717, part of the complex was used instead as a prison. Its first prominent inmate was Alexey, a son of Peter the Great.

The main entrance to this imposing fortress is Peter's Gate, a triumphal arch in the early Baroque style, which was also designed by Trezzini. It is flanked by two figures—to the right, the observant visitor will notice a statue of Minerva, the god-

dess of wisdom, and to the left stands Bellona, the goddess of war. Above the archway is the two-headed Russian eagle.

Controversial monument

Within the fortified walls, there are other well-preserved buildings. The former engineer's house contains an exhibition of family life in St Petersburg. The Commander's house also serves as a branch of the historical museum. The small boathouse within the complex once housed Peter's first sailing boat; a souvenir shop now occupies the pavilion.

In 1972, the memorial to Peter the Great near the Cathedral of Peter and Paul, which is also situated within the fortress complex, caused major controversy. In his statue of the Tsar, Russian sculptor Mikhail Shemyakin made the head much too small in relation to the body and this distorted representation caused feelings to run high.

View of the exterior of the Peter and Paul Fortress on Hare Island. The gigantic defense wall was built as a protection against Sweden in the Great Northern War (1700–1721) (above, left).

The memorial to Peter the Great sparked a great deal of discussion. The head is tiny in relation to the rest of the body (above, right).

The cannon points symbolically to the tower of the Cathedral of Peter and Paul, but it never became necessary to defend the fortress (left).

107

The last resting-place of the Tsars

Since Peter the Great, all the Tsars have been buried in the Cathedral of Peter and Paul

ADDRESS:
Petropavlovskaya
Krepost

STYLE:
Petersburg Baroque

OPENING TIMES:
Daily 11 a.m.-5 p.m.,
Tuesday 11 a.m.-4 p.m.,
Closed Weds

GETTING THERE:
Metro: Gorkovskaya;
Bus: 46; Tram: 2, 40

The last great act of state in honor of a Tsar took place in St Petersburg on the July 17, 1998, when the last Tsar, Nicholas II, who was murdered in Ekaterinburg, was laid to rest in this cathedral. Eighty years after his death, he and the rest of his murdered family were buried here alongside the remains of all the other Tsars, who had ruled the country after St Petersburg became the capital of the Russian Empire.

A burial chapel was added, in which the remains of many grand dukes are interred. The last burial here took place in 1992 when Prince Vladimir Romanov, who died in Miami, was laid to rest here with great ceremony.

The church is one of the most famous landmarks in St Petersburg. Its gilt needle-like spire soars more than 400ft (122 m) in height and is topped by the city's guardian angel, holding aloft a 23-ft (7-m) high cross.

Until the television tower was built, the church, commissioned by Peter the Great, was the tallest build-ing in the city. The Peter and Paul Cathedral owes its impressive size to the Swiss architect Domenico Trezzini, who designed it and supervised its construction in the middle of the fortress complex between 1712 and 1733. In so doing, he replaced a wooden church, which had been built there at the beginning of the 18th century.

Trezzini's design took the form of an early Baroque-style church, relatively simple on the exterior, 210ft (64 m) in length and 98ft (30m) wide, and echoing the style of west European churches.

The interior is divided into three naves, separated by pillars. The walls are decorated with frescoes, ornaments and stucco work.

The Peter and Paul Cathedral differs from other Russian-Orthodox churches in so far as it has a chancel, which was only used once for the purpose for which it was intended: in 1902 the excommunication of Leo Tolstoy, the well-known revolutionary leader, was proclaimed from this pulpit. His novel Resurrection, published a short while earlier, was regarded as open criticism of the Orthodox religion.

Of particular note is the gilded iconostasis begun in 1722 in the traditional Russian Baroque style. It resembles a triumphal arch and is a symbolic reminder of victory over Sweden in the Great Northern War. Another important landmark in the history of the church involves Telushkin, a simple laborer, whose story is still related in St Petersburg to this day. When a bolt of lightning threatened to dislodge the angel from the top of the spire, Telushkin boldly climbed up the tower and re-secured the angel.

For this act of bravery, he received money, clothing and allegedly a golden cup, which guaranteed him free drinks in all St Petersburg's taverns. According to legend, he died a few years later from drinking too much vodka.

The interior of the Cathedral is decorated with wall frescoes, ornaments and stucco work (opposite, left).

The spire of the Peter and Paul Cathedral soars to a height of almost 400ft (123m) (right).

The building is breath-takingly beautiful, especially at night (center).

The main entrance with its arrangement of pillars is also a magnif-icent sight (opposite, right).

A shining palace

The **WINTER PALACE** is the city's most famous building and is visited by 3 million tourists each year

St Petersburg
Russia
Moscow

ADDRESS:
Dvortsovaya
Naberezhnaya 32

OPENING TIMES:
10.30 a.m.-5 p.m., Sun
10.30 a.m.-4 p.m.,
Closed Mon

GETTING THERE:
Metro: Kanal
Griboyedova, Nevsky
Prospect, Gostinyi Dvor;
Bus: 7; Express Bus: 7,
10, 147; Mini Bus: 128,
129, 228; Trolley: 1, 7, 10

The Winter Palace is a masterpiece of Baroque splendor, one of the largest palaces in Europe and the most famous building in St Petersburg. Its fame is not, however, due to its external appearance, but to the fact that its monumental walls and various annexes house one of the greatest museums in the world—the Hermitage Museum.

Peter died in his palace

The first buildings began to take shape in 1711, during the reign of Peter the Great, along the Neva River, between the Admiralty and the Summer Garden. It was here in the original Winter Palace, a much more modest structure in those days, that the famous Tsar ended his days.

The colossal green and white façades of this magnificent edifice, as we see it today, are in fact the fourth version of the building. Under Elizabeth I, it was remodeled in 1762 with numerous pillars and rich ornamentation. Architect Bartolomeo Francesco Rastrelli's design became a monument to his achievements. The building complex, which is grouped around a square inner courtyard, contains more than 1,000 rooms. The sumptuous throne room, the main staircase and the palace church were designed by Rastrelli whilst the rest of the interior work was spread over the course of time between other famous architects, such as Felten, Quarenghi, Rossi, Montferrand and Stassov.

Catherine's residence

When she came to power, Catherine the Great made the Winter Palace her official residence. The interior reached the peak of its splendor during her reign. The precious white and gold Jordan staircase, the ballroom, covering an area of $11,840\text{ft}^2$ $(1,100\text{m}^2)$ and the vast Heraldic Hall are just some of the palace splendors with which the German-born monarch surrounded herself.

The first art collection

Catherine started off the original Hermitage collection in 1764 with 225 paintings, which she bought from a Berlin merchant. During her lifetime, the collection grew to 4,000 paintings, including works by Rembrandt, Rubens, Titian and Raphael. They soon filled wall after wall of the Winter Palace.

Over the centuries, this magnificent building has had to weather a number of disasters. Following a devastating fire in 1837, it required restoration on a massive scale. In October 1917, it was stormed by Lenin's Red Guards when they seized power. The building also suffered considerable damage during World War II.

Since reconstruction first began in 1950, the renovation work has not ceased, nor has the stream of visitors; each year, 3 million tourists pass through its doors.

Behind its magnificent façade, the Winter Palace has witnessed history being made. Originally, it was the home of the Tsars and then, after the October Revolution, it was the seat of the first Soviet Council. Nowadays, the Russian flag flies above the Hermitage Museum (above).

Every detail is spectacular–such as this gateway, which opens onto Palace Square (opposite).

The Palace is especially stunning when seen at night (left).

Over 3 million visitors a year come to marvel at the treasures of the Hermitage (right and below).

The two-headed eagle was the symbol of the Tsars (opposite, top).

The exhibition halls contain exceptional treasures from the days of the Tsar, such as this gilded throne (opposite, bottom).

Extraordinary exhibits

In the Hermitage Museum's 353 rooms, visitors can marvel over exquisite art treasures from the Stone Age to today

Boris Piotrovsky, who was director of the museum for many years, once estimated that "it would take 70 years to look—even briefly—at every exhibit in the Hermitage."

From the Stone Age to the present, this enormous collection comprises magnificent works from all over the world. The collection is divided into six departments to make it easier to find one's way around and computer animations help visitors find their way through the labyrinth of halls, rooms and stairwells.

The six departments

The period of Prehistoric culture, which focuses particularly on artefacts from the time of the Scythians (700–300 BC), is followed by the epoch of classical antiquity up to around 400 AD. The highlight of this department is the legendary Tauride Venus. There is also a vast number of treasures from the mysterious East, particularly in the Egyptian collection. The numismatic section boasts 90,000 coins, medals and seals. The exhibition of native art is small by comparison, the major portion of it being housed in the Russian Museum.

The painting gallery in the west European section has several stunning masterpieces and is the main showpiece of the Hermitage Museum. Old Masters such as Leonardo da Vinci, Rembrandt, El Greco and Watteau are represented here as well as Impressionists ranging from Monet to Matisse. The only thing you will not find here is contemporary art.

ADDRESS:
Dvortsovaya
Naberezhnaya 32

OPENING TIMES:
Daily 10.30 a.m.–5 p.m.,
Sun 10.30 a.m.–4 p.m.,
Closed Mon

GETTING THERE:
Metro: Kanal
Griboyedova, Nevsky
Prospect, Gostinyi Dvor;
Bus: 7; Express Bus: 7,
10, 147; Mini Bus: 128,
129, 147, 228; Trolleys: 1,
7, 10

The Hermitage—probably no other museum in the world has a name so inappropriate as that of Russia's greatest art gallery. Translated, the word means "solitary retreat." Nothing could be more inaccurate, given the throng of visitors who gather each day as the gates open.

The word "hermitage" was the name formerly given to an intimate dining chamber, of the sort found primarily in pavilions where, after dining, the tables could be pulled back in order to make more room for dancing.

Catherine the Great is reputed to have hung her first paintings in just such a room in the Winter Palace. Even before her death, however, the Winter Palace had become too small to display all the works the Tsarina had collected.

During the second half of the 18th century, two buildings were added on by the architects Felten and Vallin de la Motte—these were known as the Small and the Old Hermitage.

Together with the New Hermitage, which was added after the fire of 1837, this group of buildings has combined to form a museum of superlatives. Of the over 1,000 rooms, 353 are open to visitors. The first time that ordinary folk who were not members of the nobility were admitted to view the imperial collection was in 1852.

A total of 2.7 million exhibits

This collection of art, which had already increased enormously under a succession of tsars and tsarinas, grew even further in the aftermath of the October Revolution. Thousands of works, seized primarily from aristocratic households, were absorbed into the collection. New acquisitions are still arriving to this day and the number of exhibits has now risen to 2.7 million—ten times more than the Louvre's collection in Paris.

Inevitably, only a small percentage of items can be put on display at any given time.

The General Staff Building is one of the most impressive sights in Palace Square (right).

The spectacular Alexander Column commemorates the great victory over Napoleon's armies (below, right).

Visitors occasionally get the opportunity to admire an ice sculpture of the Winter Palace (below, left).

ADDRESS:
Dvortsovaya Ploshtad; on the southern side of the Hermitage

OPENING TIMES:
Weds to Sun between 12 a.m. and 6 p.m.

GETTING THERE:
Metro: Griboyedova Canal, Nevsky Prospect, Gostinyi Dvor;

Bus: 7; Express Bus: 7, 10, 147; Mini bus: 128, 129, 147, 228; Trolleys: 1, 7, 10

A turning point in history

Palace Square is not only a beautiful square in St Petersburg but also where the October Revolution began

St Petersburg was never a place to disguise its charms. People here like to indulge in superlatives, particularly when it comes to Palace Square. St Petersburg residents refer to it with complete assurance as the "most beautiful place in the world."

Breathtaking architecture

The architecture in St Petersburg is truly breathtaking: the Winter Palace and Hermitage border Palace Square on the River Neva side. The staff buildings of the Guards' Regiment and the Glinka Chapel with its unique acoustics are also situated here. No other place in Russia represents such a powerful symbol of the splendor and downfall of the Tsars.

Palace Square took on its present-day appearance in the 19th century, when Tsar Alexander commissioned the architect Carlo Rossi to redesign it. In 1834 the Alexander Column, which commemorates the victory over Napoleon and symbolizes one of Russia's greatest triumphs, was erected in the heart of St Petersburg. It is 157ft (48m) in height and is topped by the figure of an angel bearing a 20-ft (6-m) high cross.

Bloody Sunday

Just a few decades later, however, instead of celebrating glorious deeds by the Tsar, the Square witnessed one of the darkest chapters in Russian history, known as "Bloody Sunday." On January 9, 1905, Father Georgi Gapon, a priest, organized an assembly of 20,000 men, women and children to march to Palace Square in order to present a petition to the Tsar asking for better working conditions. Even though the crowds sang "God Protect the Tsar," the ruler had the protesters gunned down. One thousand people were killed or wounded. It was the last time the Romanovs were able to defend the throne by means of force for the seed of revolution had been sown. Although the Tsar was cheered in Palace Square in 1914 at the outbreak of World War I, by 1917 the autocratic rule of the tsars was at an end. In February of that year, following mass demonstrations, Nicholas II was forced to abdicate and hand over power to a democratic people's provisional government.

In October, the Square witnessed a great turning point in Russian history when Lenin, newly returned from exile, led the "Storm on the Winter Palace." This armed uprising by the Red Brigadists toppled the people's government on October 26th and Lenin inaugurated the first Soviet Government in the Winter Palace. During the decades that followed, the event was always celebrated with great pomp in this historic setting.

The birth of a navy

Peter the Great built Russia's first warships in the Admiralty; this former dockyard is now a naval college

St Petersburg
Russia
Moscow

ADDRESS:
Admiralteyskaya
Nabereshnaya 2

OPENING TIMES:
The building is home to a naval college and is unfortunately not open to visitors.

GETTING THERE:
Bus: 7, 10; Trolleys: 1, 5, 7, 10, 17, 22

Peter found himself facing a dilemma. On land, Russia was already a world power, but on water it was defenseless against attack—especially by the Scandinavians. While visiting the West as a young man—the first Tsar to do so—he developed a particular fascination for Holland. He was impressed not only by its architecture, but also by its mighty fleet. Traveling incognito, the Tsar learnt the techniques of shipbuilding firsthand, certain in the knowledge that without a navy Russia's future would be in great jeopardy.

A base for the first fleet
The decision to create St Petersburg was partly based on this realization. In establishing a new capital, the Tsar was keen to create not only an architectural showpiece, but also a strategic base for his navy.

To this end, work began in 1704 on a dockyard, almost at the same time as construction began on the Peter and Paul Fortress. He chose a site opposite Vassilyevskiy Island, a very deep part of the Neva river.

The work was soon completed and the first frigate to be built inside this U-shaped shipyard was successfully launched. By the time of Peter's death in 1725, a total of 262 warships had been launched and the basis for Russia's naval power was in place.

As befits its importance, the Admiralty, the new building we see today, was situated at the geographical center of St Petersburg at that time. Three great avenues radiate outward from a point in front of the Admiralty.

The building was designed by Adrian Zakharov in the style of Alexandrian classicism and construction work began in 1806. The main part of the building measures 1,335ft (407m) in length and is flanked by two wings, each 535ft (163m) long. Its focal point is the tower with its gilded spire, underneath which runs a great archway. A relief by Trebenyev depicts Neptune, god of the sea, presenting Peter I with his trident. Numerous sculptures portray military heroes such as Achilles and Alexander the Great or symbolize the

four elements. A statue is also dedicated to the Egyptian goddess Isis, the protector of shipbuilding.

One of St Petersburg's landmarks is the 236-ft (72-m) tall spire, which is only distinguishable from the spire of the Peter and Paul Cathedral by its weather vane.

From shipyard to school
By the beginning of the 19th century, the Admiralty was no longer the center of shipbuilding and had lost its significance as a fortress. Instead, the original buildings were taken over by the Ministry of the Navy and assumed importance as stately official buildings. Since 1925, a naval college has been based here. A small park, known as Alexander Park, was created along its southern façade to commemorate Peter the Great's 200th birthday.

Karl Marx later remarked in his caustic way that "Peter the Great wanted to turn a nation of land rats into a nation of water rats." Given the might of Russia's naval power today, one can only acknowledge that he succeeded.

Not only is the Admiralty one of the loveliest buildings in the city but it is also one of the oldest (above, left).

The tower is built in the same style as the Peter and Paul Cathedral (above, right).

The gates of this famous building once enclosed Russia's first shipyard. Peter the Great's warships were built here (left).

Architectural masterpiece

KAZAN CATHEDRAL, modeled on St Peter's Basilica in Rome, has a distinctive stone colonnade

ADDRESS:
Kazanskaya Ploshchad 2

STYLE:
Classicism

SERVICES:
Daily 10 a.m.–6 p.m.

GETTING THERE:
Metro: Nevsky Prospect, Gostiny Dvor; Bus: 3, 7, 22, 27; Trolleys: 1, 5, 7, 10, 17, 22

Towards the end of the 19th century, Tsar Paul I, aware that death was imminent, was gripped by a fervent desire that his native city should be graced with a church modeled on St Peter's Basilica in Rome. He chose Russian architect Andrey Voronikhin to construct the building. It is to him that the city owes the Cathedral of Our Lady of Kazan, the design of which was to serve as a model for many other buildings throughout the world.

The architect was faced with a difficult dilemma: the chosen site for the new church was one of the city's main boulevards, the Nevsky Prospect, which runs from east to west. According to Orthodox tradition, however, the central nave and altar must face east. At the same time, the building's imposing façade had to face out onto the Nevsky Prospect, which would have meant that the church would mainly have been viewed from its—usually less attractive—side elevation rather than from the front.

Exemplary architecture

Andrey Voronikhin hit upon a bold solution to the problem: he designed a magnificent semicircular colonnade in front of the side elevation, the center of which is the entrance to the cathedral. This curving colonnade with its imposing Corinthian columns forms Kazan Square. In this way, all the criteria were met: the church faced east, the entrance was appropriately imposing and its appearance was reminiscent of St Peter's Basilica in Rome.

This architectural achievement is echoed inside the church. Built in the style of Alexandrian, the cross-shaped main body of the church resembles a palatial-style hall with double rows of pillars.

The cathedral takes its name from what was once its most valuable asset, the miracle-making icon of Our Lady of Kazan. Peter brought it to St Petersburg from Moscow in 1710, but it went missing during the centuries that followed.

Tribute to a national hero

The church was undergoing construction during the time of the Napoleonic War. One of the country's heroes in this war was the commander of the Russian army, General Field Marshal Mikhail Kutosov. On October 18, 1812, he won a decisive victory in which he drove Napoleon's *grande armée* out of Moscow. After his death, he was interred in the north wing of Kazan Cathedral.

It is one of the paradoxes of history that the Soviets chose this of all cathedrals to serve as a "Museum of Atheism." Services have since been resumed in Kazan Cathedral.

Not only is Kazan Cathedral famed for its beauty as a church but it is also known for its impressive colonnade.

Peter the Great, triumphant

To mark the hundredth birthday of the city's founder, Catherine commissioned a statue to be erected in what is now Decembrists Square

ADDRESS:
Ploshchad Dekabristov, in the center on the River Neva

GETTING THERE:
By bus: 3, 22, 27;
Trolleys: 5, 22

St Petersburg in the December of 1825: the long, dark days of winter have arrived in the North and descended upon the city when a sad piece of news reaches the townsfolk. Tsar Alexander I has died unexpectedly without leaving a legitimate heir to the throne. Behind the scenes at the Winter Palace, a bitter power struggle to find a successor is in progress. In particular, a group of noble officers, the Decembrists, decide to seize their opportunity. Their leader was Prince Volkonskiy, who had been conspiring for some time with various secret societies against the outdated, archaic ruling system. During their various military campaigns, he and his soldiers had realized just how backward Russia was in comparison to its Western neighbors. Hence the attempted coup.

When Alexander's brother Nicholas was named as the new Tsar on December 14th, 3,000 soldiers refused to swear an oath of allegiance to the new ruler and marched in protest to what was one of the most popular squares in the city, Peter's Square.

The crowd of predominantly young men pleaded loudly and passionately for an end to serfdom and autocratic rule. The new Tsar responded with gunfire, bringing the insurrection to a bloody end in order to keep himself in power.

The leaders of the putsch were arrested and imprisoned in the Fortress of Peter and Paul. A year later, Prince Volkonskiy and his fellow officer conspirators were executed while other insurgents were banished to Siberia.

Late recognition

One hundred years later, those involved in the uprising were honored by the Communist regime. In 1925, the scene of the uprising, formerly known as "Senate Square" and later, as "Peter's Square," was renamed "Decembrists Square." This large area is situated next to the Admiralty on the Neva. The western side of this landscaped square is dominated by the triumphal arch of the Senate and Synod. This yellow and white build-ing with its loggias and Corinthian columns was begun in 1829 and designed by architect Carlo Rossi. Its group of "Justice and Piety" sculptures which adorn the building symbolize the unity of temporal and church power.

The monument to Peter the Great stands majestically in the center of the square; it is also known as the "Bronze Horseman" after a famous poem by Pushkin. Catherine the Great commissioned it in 1782 in Peter's honor. The inscription which reads "Peter the First, Catherine the Second" serves to underline Catherine's equal status.

The stone monolith from the Gulf of Finland, on which the statue sits, weighs 1,763 tons (1,600 metric tons) and the bronze figure is the work of Etienne-Maurice Falconet. Peter, the dynamic ruler, is depicted gazing self-assuredly towards the Neva. His rearing horse is trampling a snake, the symbol of deceit.

Catherine the Great commissioned the memorial in Decembrists Square to mark Peter the Great's 100th birthday. It depicts the legendary Tsar, pointing with outstretched hand. His horse is trampling a snake–the symbol of deceit. Transporting the giant monolith, on which the statue stands, from the Gulf of Finland to the heart of the city was a monumental feat.

Power embodied in stone

The gigantic Cathedral of St Isaac dwarfs even the largest of the Tsar's palaces

ADDRESS:
Isaakievskaya
Ploshchad

OPENING TIMES:
Museum: Daily 10.30
a.m.-8 p.m.;
Observation walkway:
Daily 10.30 a.m.-7 p.m.,
closed Weds;
Cathedral: Daily 11
a.m.-7 p.m., Closed
Weds

GETTING THERE:
Metro: Nevsky Prospect,
Gostiny Dvor; Bus: 22;
Trolleys: 5, 22

Monumental buildings always convey a message. St Isaac's Cathedral in St Petersburg dominates the skyline: its dome, which soars to a height of over 328ft (100m), towers above all the rest of the Tsar's palaces. Yet however forcefully this gleaming gold dome emphasizes the superior position of the temporal rulers, the gigantic cathedral is a symbol of who is supreme above all things.

Impressive facts

The dimensions of this building are extremely impressive in themselves—measuring 365ft (111m) in length and 318ft (97m) in breadth, the church towers to a height of 335ft (101.5m). It took almost 40 years—from 1818 to 1858—to complete with 11,000 serfs working under extremely difficult conditions. The marshy ground proved a statistical challenge: 24,000 wooden piles were needed to provide this imposing cathedral with a solid foundation.

All the efforts eventually proved worthwhile, however: the dome itself, decorated with several hundred kilograms of gold leaf, is a major attraction and a distinctive landmark on St Petersburg's skyline.

The fascinating nature of this architectural masterpiece becomes even clearer if one views the building as a whole: constructed of red granite and gray marble, the cathedral is built to a rectangular ground-plan. The most outstanding features of its stunning exterior are the main entrances, which are modeled on the Roman Pantheon. Three rows of 16 columns, each 55ft (17m) high, invite the visitor into the breathtaking nave of the church, where one's gaze is immediately drawn to the stylishly decorated bronze reliefs that decorate the area above the columns. The main dome has a diameter of 85ft (26m), is topped by a small cupola supported by eight pillars and surrounded by four smaller bell towers.

Ornate interior

Three great bronze doors lead into the interior, which measures 43,055 ft^2 (4,000m^2) and is lit by 12 windows in the dome. The ceilings and walls are decorated with paintings and mosaics, for which a total of 43 different types of minerals and colored stone were used.

The ceiling fresco under the main dome forms the spectacular central feature of the building. This work of

The cathedral's mighty dome, which rises over 328ft (100m) in height, is one of the largest of its kind (opposite, bottom left).

As illustrated by this door, every detail of decoration is magnificent (opposite, bottom right).

The fresco up in the dome depicting Mary surrounded by angels is the cathedral's artistic star attraction (left).

The building is also a spectacular sight at night (below).

art depicting the Mother of God surrounded by apostles, evangelists and saints, was created by Bruellov, an artist of the Russian Academy. The glass window in the sanctuary comes from Munich and depicts the Resurrection of Christ.

Two earlier versions of the church had already been completed by the early 18th century, but the Russian Tsarist family was not quite satisfied with their dimensions. It was not until 1818 that the French architect, Auguste de Montferrand, remodeled St Isaac's Cathedral to its current monumental size.

Magnificent view

The cathedral was sanctified in 1858 and named after a Byzantine monk, Isaak von Dalmation, patron saint of Peter the Great. It incorporates an observation walkway, one of the highest in all St Petersburg. This can be reached by climbing 262 steps to reach the gallery beneath the dome, where the visitor is rewarded with a magnificent view across the city to the Fortress of Peter and Paul, the Admiralty and the Winter Palace.

Services in the cathedral were banned after the 1917 Revolution, but were finally resumed in 1990.

A fairy-tale cathedral

The Church of the Resurrection was built by Tsar Alexander III in Old-Russian style as a symbol of power

St Petersburg
Russia
Moscow

ADDRESS:
Nab. Kanala
Griboyedova 2b

OPENING TIMES:
Mon, Tues, Thurs to
Sun
11 a.m.-6 p.m.

GETTING THERE:
Buslines 3, 7, 22, 27;
Trolley 1, 5, 7, 10, 22

In the center of St Petersburg stands the Church of the Resurrection, a building that jars slightly in contrast with the predominantly Western, European style of most other buildings in the city center. Its gleaming blue and gold cupolas, which are best viewed from the large Marsfeld Park, give it a distinctly oriental appearance.

A breath of the Orient
Surrounded by a more Classical style of architecture, this church is more like something borrowed from the Arabian Nights. Its ornately decorated windows, colorful cupolas and elaborate ornamentation combine to lure the visitor into a fairytale world.

The superb beauty of the mosaics and the large, striking portrait of Christ on the main façade are particularly worthy of mention and were designed by well-known Russian painters.

The architects used 20 different types of colored stone to create this artistic ensemble, which covers an area of 75,347ft^2 (7,000m^2). The cathedral is often thought to be much older than it actually is. The building, which is

also known as "Church of the Savior on the Spilled Blood" as well as just "Savior Church" or "Blood Church," is actually of more recent construction than the surrounding historical buildings. Although it gives the impression of having stood for at least a 1,000 years, it was only completed toward the end of the 19th century.

Memorial to a Tsar
Tsar Alexander III had the church erected in memory of his father Alexander II, who died in March 1881, the victim of a bomb attack near the Griboyedov canal. The attack was the work of "People's Will," a secret revolutionary group which hoped to bring about the reform of the country's antiliberal regime.

The conspirators' hopes were dashed, however, as the assassination did not lead to any changes in the country. On the contrary, the new Tsar Alexander ruled with a rod of iron and continued unwaveringly on the same course. His plans for a new church, which turned the site of the murder into a memorial, served to underline his determination in this respect.

A demonstration of power
The Tsar commissioned a monumental building, intended as an unequivocal show of power. Moscow's St Basil Cathedral served as the model for the new building, and its traditional Russian style was intended to reflect the conservative nature of his rule. By focusing on traditional Russian architecture, Tsar Alexander was at the same time veering away from what he saw as too much contaminating Western influence.

After two years in the planning, this spectacular church was constructed between 1883 and 1907 and from then on was, in the eyes of the Orthodox Church, a symbol of Orthodox faith under the Tsarist empire.

Following the October Revolution, the Savior Cathedral, like many other churches in Russia, was desanctified and no longer used for worship. In the 1960s, its value as a cultural asset was rediscovered and today the cathedral has emerged from 30 years of renovation work in all its new splendor. Since 1997, as the Museum of Russian Mosaic, it is once again one of the most-visited tourist attractions in the city.

The traditional Russian architectural style of the Cathedral of the Resurrection provides a vivid splash of color between the Classical-style buildings. The onion-shaped domes look particularly splendid at night (above, left).

The towers are modeled unmistakably on those of St Basil's Cathedral in Moscow's Red Square (above, right).

The size and traditional Russian style of architecture of the cathedral are clearly intended as symbols of the Tsar's power (left).

Center of the fine arts

Russia's great painters learned their trade at the ACADEMY OF ARTS on Vassilyevskiy Island

ADDRESS:
Universitetskaya
Naberezhnaya 7

OPENING TIMES:
Daily 11 a.m.-6 p.m.,
Closed Mon and
Tuesday

GETTING THERE:
Metro:
Vassileostrovskaya; Bus:
7, 47; Tram: 11

The Academy of Arts has produced important painters, sculptors and architects—the early neoclassical style building is itself a work of art.

Teachers as architects

This famous academy was founded by Tsarina Elizabeth I in 1757, but the imposing building was not completed until 30 years later. Designed by Jean Baptiste Vallin de la Mothe and Alexander Kokorinov, both of whom were teachers at the academy, it was constructed on University Quay. Yuriy Felten also became involved in its construction in 1780. Its superb central courtyard, measuring 130ft (40m) in diameter, is particularly impressive.

The wings and the side which faces the gardens are built in strict Classical style while the façade that fronts onto the Neva with its statues of Hercules and Flora reveals a distinct Baroque influence. On the river side a large, sweeping staircase leads up to the halls of the academy, which were added by Konstantin Thon around 1830.

The entrance is flanked by what are probably the oldest works of art in St Petersburg: two mighty sphinxes rest on massive granite bases. Each one measures 12ft (3.60m) in height, 16ft (5m) in length and weighs 25 tons (23 metric tons). They represent Pharaoh Amenophis III and date from 1400 BC. Excavated in about 1820 in Thebes, these fabulous mythical statues were purchased by Tsar Nicholas I in 1832. It took almost a year to transport them from the Nile to the Neva.

Where art history was written

Art history was written within the rooms of the academy. It was here that Russian artists began—in creative terms—to break away from the Middle Ages and turn toward Western forms of artistic expression.

Architects such as Voronikhin and Zakharov, sculptors including Clodt von Juergensburg and Anikushin studied and taught here, along with painters, such as Ivanov, Brodsky and Repin.

Repin as model

The university is now named after Ilya J. Repin (1844–1930), the most significant exponent of Russian realism and one of the country's most prominent artists. His powerful works, including *The Barge Haulers on the Volga*, cemented his international reputation. He was also an extremely influential member of the "Peredvishniki" artistic reform movement toward the end of the 19th century.

Repin's most important paintings are on display in the Russian Museum of St Petersburg and the Tretyakov Gallery in Moscow.

Contemporary art

The historic grounds of the Academy of Arts are also home to a museum which exhibits works by members of the academy and holds numerous special exhibitions featuring works by foreign artists. In contrast to other famous museums in the city, works of contemporary art are also on display here. In the wake of the political upheavals, Russia has witnessed the development of a young, wild, dynamic art movement, which has gained international recognition.

There are also 26 panels commemorating famous scientists, who lived and worked here. The apartment belonging to Ivan Pavlov, the 1904 Nobel Prize winner for Medicine, has been preserved as a small exhibition area.

The flights of steps lead up to the academy's teaching rooms where painters such as Repin learned their trade (above, left).

The academy building, founded by Catherine the Great, is attractively situated on Vassilyevskiy Island (above, right).

The sphinx is one of the city's oldest cultural treasures. It stands outside the Academy of Arts (left).

The monastery that never was

SMOLNY CLOISTER once educated the daughters of aristocratic families. Then the Soviets came to power. Today, it is the seat of the city's mayor

ADDRESS:
Ploshchad Rastrelli 3/1

OPENING TIMES:
Daily 11 a.m.-5 p.m.,
Closed Thursday

GETTING THERE:
Metro: Chernyshevskaya;
Bus: 22, 134, 136;
Trolley: 15, 49

The word "*Smolny*," the name of this "cloister" in the eastern part of St Petersburg, sounds almost poetic to Western ears. The translation, however, is rather disillusioning: "*smolny*" is in fact the Russian word for "tar." This black, viscous material was produced here during the reign of Peter I for use in his shipyards. This foul-smelling place was turned into an attractive area when Elizabeth I decided in 1748 to establish a nunnery on the site, where she planned to spend her final years.

Once again, it was her favorite architect, Rastrelli, who was responsible for the construction of the cloister complex. At its center stands the Church of the Resurrection, which he designed in typical Russian Baroque style. Finished in blue, white and gold, this church with its clusters of pillars and ornamented windows is reminiscent in style of Catherine's Palace in Tzarskoje Selo, another of Rastrelli's masterpieces. The main tower rises to 308ft (94m) and provides an excellent view over the whole of St Petersburg.

Elizabeth died before the cloister was completed. The nuns' cells, which were built in a square around the church, were not completed until the 19th century and were never used as accommodation for nuns.

The ballroom as a venue for the Soviet Congress

Catherine the Great later founded the Smolny Institute on the site in 1764. This was the first college in Russia to cater for aristocratic young women.

The education of these upper-class young girls came to an abrupt end when workers' and soldiers' councils took over the building in August 1917. Lenin set up living and working quarters for himself in the cloister. In October 1917, an all-Russian Soviet Congress was held in the ballroom where these aristocratic young girls had once danced with officers of the Tsar's army.

The Soviet Government had its seat in the Smolny Institute until the center of power was transferred to Moscow. In 1923, two of the gateway arches were inscribed with the legendary motto: "Proletarians of all nations unite!" Ten years later, Stalin was planning his brutal purges. The building remained in the hands of the CPSU until 1991 and is now the official seat of the mayor of St Petersburg and the city administration.

Elizabeth I built Smolny Cloister with the intention of spending her final years there. She died before it was finished and the nuns never took up residence. It is now the seat of the mayor of St Petersburg and his administration.

A palatial church

The ST NICHOLAS NAVAL CATHEDRAL looks as if it is actually part of Catherine's Palace

ADDRESS:
Nikolskaya Ploshchad 1-3

STYLE:
Baroque

SERVICES:
Daily 10 a.m.–6 p.m.

GETTING THERE:
Metro: Sadovaya /
Sennaya Ploshchad; Bus
3, 22, 27 from Nevsky
Prospect

Anyone seeing the lavishly decorated and picturesque St Nicholas Naval Cathedral for the first time could be forgiven for thinking that they have landed in the wrong place: with its blue and white, richly decorated exterior, the building, situated close to the Krukyov Canal, bears a striking resemblance to Catherine's Palace in Tsarskoye Selo.

The startling similarity in architectural styles is no coincidence: the church was constructed between 1753 and 1762 by Savva Chevakinsky, an enthusiastic pupil of the Italian architect Francesco Rastrelli, who was responsible for the sumptuous appearance of Catherine's Palace.

Church and bell tower

The church is built in the shape of a Greek cross. This simple shape is complicated, however, by projections in the façade and clusters of pillars at each corner. Stucco work adorns the windows and gilded towers soar upward. Russian-Orthodox tradition dictates that every church has five of these graceful structures.

What is unusual about this particular church is that it has a free-standing bell tower situated at a distance of 328ft (100m) from the main church. It forms a prominent landmark indicating the site of the cathedral in the heart of the city. Situated in what was formerly the sailors' quarters, the church was named after St Nicholas, patron saint of mariners.

Naval memorial church

Daily services are held in the eerily dark lower part of the church on the ground floor. Orthodox services were permitted in this church even during the Communist era. St Nicholas' Naval Cathedral was a place where relatives of killed or drowned sailors could come to express their grief. Memorial services were held here, for example, for the crews of sunken submarines. The cathedral also contains a commemorative plaque in their memory.

Valuable iconostasis

On special occasions, the magnificent, brightly-lit upper church is used for services on the occasion of church festivals. The upper church also contains the cathedral's most valuable sacred object: a lavishly decorated iconostasis dating from the 18th century. The middle part, the Holy Gate, is only opened on festival days.

The Cathedral's blue and white, richly decorated façade is distinctly reminiscent of the Winter Palace (above).

The bell tower is situated about 328ft (100m) away from the church itself (opposite, far left).

The gates to St Nicholas Naval Cathedral were among the few that remained open to the faithful during the Soviet regime–it was a place to mourn naval crewmen who had been killed or drowned (center).

The golden cupola of the bell tower can be seen from all over the city (left).

Murder of a tyrant

Paul I tyrannized his people. Fearing assassination, he built the **MIKHAILOVSKY PALACE**, but it proved unable to save him

ADDRESS:
Sadovaya Uliza 2

OPENING TIMES:
Daily 10 a.m.-5 p.m.,
Mon 10 a.m.- 4 p.m.,
Closed Tuesday

GETTING THERE:
Metro: Nevsky Prospect,
Gostiny Dvor; Bus: 46;
Tram: 2

Being the Tsar and ruler of Russia was a dangerous job at the best of times. History shows that there were always treacherous assassins—be it wife, friend or enemy—among the ruler's immediate entourage. The more the ruler was hated by the people, the greater was the threat to his life.

The tyrannical Tsar Paul I

Tsar Paul I was aware of this when he inherited the crown from his mother Catherine the Great. Driven by a desire to do everything as differently as possible to his hated mother, he gradually became during the course of his reign a tyrant of the worst sort. His bloody rule led Alexander Pushkin to remark that "Caligulas can be born even during enlightened times."

Paul was very conscious of his unpopularity among his subjects and many of his courtiers. He consequently lived in permanent fear of assassination.

Convinced that the palaces of St Petersburg were not safe enough, he ordered the demolition of a pleasant little palace on the river and replaced it with the Mikhailovsky Palace.

In accordance with the Tsar's instructions, the building, which was built between 1797 and 1800 to a design by Vincenzo Brenna, was more like a fortress than a residence—the original palace was surrounded by deep ditches; the four wings of the red

façade were grouped round a square inner courtyard.

A murder which provoked jubilation

The new palace proved unable to grant the tyrannical Tsar the protection he craved. Just 42 days after taking up residence in his new palace, Tsar Paul met a sudden end. In March 1801 he was brutally beaten to death in his own bedchamber. The assassination was the work of Platon Subov, the last of Catherine's lovers. His crime was left unpunished as the murder provoked a veritable storm of jubilation among the Russian people. It is rumored that Paul's son, Alexander I, also had a hand in the murder conspiracy.

The heir to the throne turned his back not only his father, but also on the new residence: Alexander, like all

the tsars who succeeded him, abandoned the Mikhailovsky Palace and again adopted the sumptuous Winter Palace as his main residence.

From fortress to museum

The building, which is attractively situated on Canal Island between the Fontanka and Moyka rivers on the one side and two canals on the other, remained unused for several years.

In 1823, it was turned into a college for army engineers, from which it derived the name "Engineers' Castle." Its most famous student was Dostoyevsky.

Fortress-like Mikhailovsky Palace stands on a small island and was once only accessible by drawbridge. The tyrannical Paul I sought to protect himself within its walls, but his assassins managed to reach him.

Journey in time

The RUSSIAN MUSEUM transports its visitors into the world of Russian art history

ADDRESS:
Inzhernernaya Uliza 4

OPENING TIMES:
Daily 10 a.m.–6 p.m.,
Mon 10 a.m.–5 p.m.,
Closed Tuesday

GETTING THERE:
Metro: Nevsky Prospect,
Gostiny Dvor; Bus: 100;
Trolley: 1, 5, 7, 10, 22

One could wander through the 120 rooms of the Russian Museum for days on end and still discover something new and interesting. Comprised of over 400,000 exhibits, it constitutes the world's largest exhibition of Russian art, with the oldest items dating from over 1,000 years ago.

A palace for art
The Mikhailovsky Palace is a magnificent building, located on the picturesque Square of Arts, and provides a fitting framework for such a remarkable exhibition. The Classical-style building was built between 1819 and 1825 by Carlo Rossi for Prince Mikhail Pavlovich, brother of Tsar Alexander I.

Inside the Palace, Rossi's large vestibule with its superb staircase and the White Room with its brightly colored ceiling frescoes have been successfully preserved. The Grand Prince formerly maintained a literary salon here. In 1898, under Nicholas II, it became the Russian Museum. An additional building, designed by Benois and known as the Benois Wing, was added to the museum in 1912. The original collection grew steadily and is now organized chronologically and by subject.

Journey in time through art history
The journey through Russia's art history begins around AD 988 with works dating from the Old Russian period. The most important art form during the period between Russia's

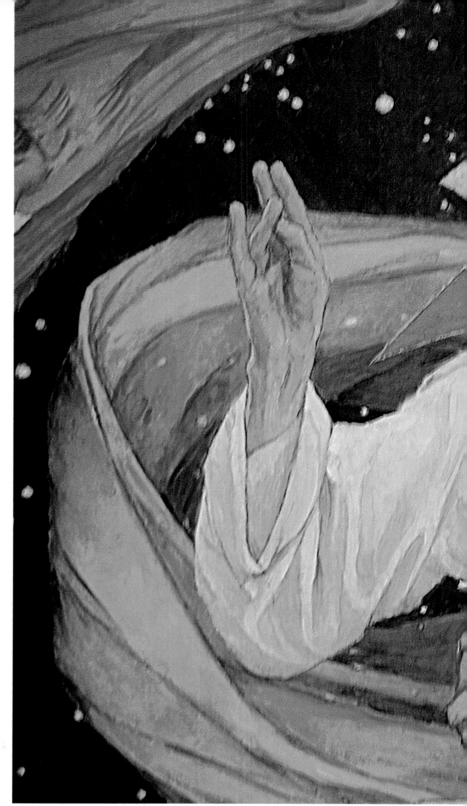

conversion to Christianity and the 17th century was iconography and in the Russian Museum you will discover a collection of superb icons spanning a period of over 700 years.

Peter the Great's reforms had a corresponding effect on the arts in Russia. Freed from ecclesiastical restraints, 18th-century art was increasingly influenced by portrait and historical painting as well as sculpture. The most significant representatives of this epoch are Ivan Nikitin, Anton Lossenko and Ivan Martos.

Ideological struggle
Early in the 19th century, Italian influences began to make themselves felt. Furthermore, the incipient struggle between opposing ideologies was beginning to be echoed in art. Landscape painting grew in importance. The most prominent artists during this epoch were Karl Bruellov, Andrey Ivanov and Sylvester Schedrin.

The late 19th century is characterized by the "Peredvishniki" movement, the most significant proponents of which include Ilya Repin and Ivan Shishkin, whose paintings explore and address themes of social injustice.

From the 1930s, socialist realism replaced Impressionism and Symbolism as the officially preferred art movement in the USSR. The stylistic criteria of socialist realism were fulfilled by painters such as Pavel Kusnezov and Petr Konchalovsky.

March of the modernist era
The fall of the Soviet government brought to an end the Russian Museum's one-sided approach to art. Since the end of the 1980s, paintings by previously reviled early 20th-century avant-garde artists, such as Kasimir Malevich, Vassily Kandinsky and Marc Chagall, have been added to the collection.

The Russian Museum highlights the development of the country's art from its earliest beginnings to the modern day. One of its most significant exhibitions is devoted to icon painting. This ancient art of painting was widely used in the decoration of palace walls (above).

The exhibits comprise drawings, paintings and even numerous sculptures, such as this figure of a woman (opposite).

Michael's Palace, which houses the main part of the collection, is built in the Classical style (left).

135

Green idyll in the center of the city

Situated in an idyllic location at the confluence of the Neva and Fontanka rivers, the **SUMMER GARDEN** is perfect for leisurely walks

ADDRESS:
Naberezhnaya Kutosova

OPENING TIMES:
Palace: May 1–Nov 10
from 11 a.m.–7 p.m.,
Closed Tues;
Garden: March–Oct
from 8 a.m.–10 p.m.

GETTING THERE:
Bus: 46; Tram: 2

St Petersburg's oldest park is also its most beautiful. For generations, the Summer Garden has provided residents and tourists alike with an opportunity to enjoy peace and tranquility in a natural setting. Tsar Peter the Great I commissioned Jean Baptiste Leblond, who also planned the Peterhof gardens, to design the park. Leblond, a talented landscape designer, originally created the Summer Garden in Baroque style. As well as feasts and fireworks, the Tsar loved water features of every kind and as a consequence, the park's walkways are lined with sculptures and numerous fountains.

Given its spectacular situation, the Summer Garden was frequently the setting for sumptuous balls and firework displays. The French-inspired layout with its straight avenues, grottos, orangery and fountains, was destroyed in a flood in 1777.

After the flood, the park was redesigned—no less splendidly—in the style of an English landscaped park. Ancient trees are surrounded by grassy areas, a small lake lies in the midst of lush greenery and an attractive teahouse invites visitors to linger a while.

The Summer Garden with its little pavilions was created during the reign of Peter the Great (opposite, top).

The sculptures, which can be seen all over the park, have also survived since this time (left and below).

The idyllic peace and tranquility is a magnet for people who want to go for a stroll and escape the stresses of everyday life for a while (opposite, bottom).

Distributed about the gardens are approximately 100 marble sculptures, which have survived since the days of Peter the Great. These elegant Italian statues mainly represent allegorical figures, but Queen Christine of Sweden, Marcus Aurelius, and Alexander the Great can also be encountered during a walk in the park.

In 1784, Yuriy Felten created a masterpiece of wrought iron work for the Summer Garden—an artistic wrought iron fence with gilded rosettes, which stretches along the bank of the Neva River and is supported by pink granite pillars.

A small residence

The palace is situated in the northern part of the garden by the river and was created between 1710 and 1714. It is one of the few surviving buildings from the time of Peter the Great. This simple, rectangular, two-story palace was designed at Peter's request by Italian architect Domenico Trezzini. The harmonious façade reliefs depicting scenes from the Great Northern War are the work of the German architect Andreas Schlüter.

The rooms on the ground floor were used by Peter for his handicraft activities while his wife Catherine occupied the first floor. It is said that when there were too many guests in the small dining room, some of them had to eat their meal standing up. The Summer Palace, which has been lovingly restored, is well worth a visit for its display of original furniture.

Beacons

Rostral columns on the **STRELKA** once were lighthouses, guiding ships into St Petersburg Harbor

LOCATION:
At the eastern tip of Vassilyevskiy Island, Stock Exchange Square

GETTING THERE:
Bus: 7, 10, 492; Trolleys: 1, 7, 10

In the fall, when the bright nights of St Petersburg give way to polar darkness, the Baltic becomes a harsh place to live. The first ice floes begin to form and a few days with below-freezing temperatures are sufficient to cause the Gulf of Finland to freeze over. What a reassuring sight it must have been for the captains of the homecoming fleet of wooden ships to see the great fire beacons signaling the port of St Petersburg on the horizon.

They were lit on top of the two Rostral columns, which rise to a height of 110ft (34m). These two former lighthouses also mark the Strel-

ka, the spit of land that runs out into the sea from Vassilyevskiy Island.

The columns, which are still lit to this day to mark special occasions, were built in 1810 by Swiss architect Thomas de Thomon and adorned with green ship's prows, known in Latin as a "*rostrum*," from which the name is derived.

Symbols of victory

These columns were built to symbolize the victories of the Russian fleet. The allegorical statues flanking the columns symbolize the rivers Neva, Volga, Dnepr and Volkhov. Like the prow of a ship, the Strelka narrows to a point in the confluence of the large and small Neva. Between 1733 and 1855, this was where the harbor was located. Today, this tranquil spot is filled with trees and flowerbeds and is regarded as the prettiest waterfront in the city. From this eastern tip of Vassilyevskiy Island, there are views in

one direction of the Peter and Paul Fortress and of the Admiralty and Winter Palace on the Imperial side of the city center in the other.

Another building to have survived in the former harbor area at the tip of Vassilyevskiy Island is the old Customs House, which now contains the Pushkin House, with its literary museum. The original packing buildings have become home to the Zoological Museum, which boasts 40,000 exhibits and is one of the largest of its kind anywhere in the world.

The Stock Exchange, built on the Spit in 1805, resembles a Classical temple and is decorated with columns and sculptures. Stocks and shares were traded here in a chamber measuring 9,687ft^2 (900m^2) up until the end of the 19th century.

The Strelka forms the
tip of Vassilyevskiy
Island, one of the most
attractive districts in St
Petersburg

A church built for a victorious navy

To honor Russia's naval victory over the Turks, Catherine commissioned several churches. The most beautiful of these is Chesme Church in St Petersburg

ADDRESS:
Uliza Lensoveta 12

STYLE:
Gothic

GETTING THERE:
Metro: Moskovskaya;
Bus: 16; Tram 35, 45

Chesme is a small port with an attractive old town in western Turkey. Nowadays, it is a popular holiday resort for foreign tourists and well-heeled residents. However, the turquoise waters of the Aegean were not always as peaceful as they are today. The war between the Russians and the Turks, which had broken out in 1768, reached its climax off this coast two years later—hence, the recurrence of the name "Chesme" in many parts of Russia.

The "Greek project"
Catherine earned the epithet "Great" not least as a result of her grand visions. One of her most ambitious goals was the so-called "Greek Project." The Tsarina dreamed of driving the infidel Ottomans out of Constantinople, or Istanbul as it is known today. Her aim was to banish the Koran from Hagia Sophia, one of the oldest churches in the history of mankind, and replace it with the liturgies of the Eastern Orthodox Church.

Reluctant to see their Russian neighbor gain too much strength in the East, the Western European pow-

ers of France, Germany and England viewed Catherine's plans with scepticism, whilst at the same time applauding her efforts against the infidels.

The naval battle of Chesme took place on June 5th under the leadership of Prince Alexey Orlov. Actively supported by English seamen, the relatively young and numerically inferior Russian fleet managed to defeat the Turks at sea. The Ottomans fled, leaving a fleet of over 20 ships anchored in the port of Chesme. Two days later, the Russians dealt with the vessels lying at anchor: 10 were captured, and the rest were sunk.

Catherine did not succeed in capturing Constantinople, but her victory over the Turks brought her valuable territory in the south. Russia finally gained what she had long coveted: access to the Black Sea and hence to the Mediterranean and Atlantic beyond.

Commemorative churches
The Tsarina was delighted with Orlov's heroic deeds and his victory at Chesme. In the years that followed, Catherine had churches and chapels,

as well as monuments, erected all over the country as an expression of her gratitude—and also as a clear signal to the Orthodox Church. One of the most beautiful of these churches is the neo-Gothic Chesme Church in St Petersburg.

A dream in salmon-pink
This extremely pretty church was built in the southern part of St Petersburg between 1777 and 1780. It was designed by architect Yuriy Felten, who envisaged the building as part of a palace complex for the Tsarina to use on her journey to Tsarskoye Selo or Pavlovsk.

Felten's design was a combination of both Gothic and Oriental elements and resulted in an extremely romantic-looking building. The façades are finished in salmon-pink and interspersed with white vertical stripes. It has an unusual exterior consisting of four semicircular apses, each crowned with a delicate small tower with a further tower positioned in the center. The result is a typical five-domed building, the filigree pointed arches of which serve to complete its picturesque appearance.

St Petersburg's picturesque Chesme Church is just one of the many churches all over Russia built by Catherine the Great to commemorate her victory. It is designed in pseudo-Gothic style.

An entire region conceived as an artistic whole

Peter the Great had visions of a Baroque architectural ensemble comprising not just a town but all the land surrounding it

ADDRESS:
Nevsky Prospect, corner of Mikhailovskaya Uliza 1/7

GETTING THERE:
Metro: Nevsky Prospect

He took a rock, and then another and in this way assembled the entire town in the air." Only then did he place it upon the earth. According to a fairy tale by Count Vladimir Odoyevsky, this is how the new capital of St Petersburg came into existence. Not only did Peter plan the town itself, he also remodeled the entire natural landscape around his new capital along Baroque guidelines.

The resulting cultural landscape extends to a distance of almost 25 miles (40km) west of the former capital as far as the Gulf of Finland. Outstanding examples of this bold plan, which was conceived on a vast scale, are the great residences that can be found all around St Petersburg.

Construction and extension work

Peter the Great began constructing this cultural landscape in 1710. It stretches from Strelna to Peerhof and Kolomna and then to Oranienbaum. His successors added numerous additional palaces and parks to his original designs, including the famous residences of Tsarskoye Selo, Gachina and Pavlovsk. Since World War II, however, many of the earlier build-

Oranienbaum Park and Palace (below), Peterhof (top right) and Strelna (lower right) are all part of the whole architectural and artistic ensemble that Peter the Great hoped to create in the north of the country.

ings have fallen victim to neglect or new building projects although others have been beautifully restored. President Valdimir Putin, for example has had Strelna Palace extended into an official state building to receive state visitors. A recent G8 summit was held here.

Ingermanland, a sparsely populated region on the Gulf of Finland, was formerly an area of largely infertile and boggy ground, covered by forests and scrub. Before commencing work on his task, the Tsar had gained inspiration from his travels in Central and Western Europe. Using Holland's dikes as his model, he had canals built that led to the Baltic. He was fascinated, in particular, by Amsterdam, which is why he ordered a shipyard, which he named *Novaya Gollandia*, to be built in Kolomna, now a district of St Petersburg. The Oranienbaum Palace is yet another example of Dutch influence.

Peter I deliberately chose locations near the sea for Oranienbaum, Strelna and Peterhof. By ensuring that the sea was permanently in view, he hoped to convert his compatriots into a nation of seafarers. As we know, the royal household was less than enthu-

siastic about transferring to a new capital and in order to make their enforced sojourn more acceptable, Peter had country estates built outside St Petersburg.

Early environmental protection

Peter was always greatly concerned with protecting the forests. To this end, he personally planted oak trees in the parks surrounding his residences. The canals and roads gradually began to be lined with houses and parks.

In just a few years, a cultural landscape had begun to take shape, a landscape comprised of country houses and parks of varying sizes which were connected by a main traffic route running along the coast This road formed a visual line linking areas of water, parks and scattered monuments, thereby creating a scenically varied artistic whole.

To encourage social intercourse between the residents of these country estates, Peter dispensed with boundary fences. Members of his royal court were expected to break with Russian traditions and adopt the European custom of paying courtesy calls on one another.

Residence of the Tsars

The **PETERHOF** offers a glimpse of the glittering lifestyle of the Tsar and his family, who lived in the midst of a magnificent park

ADDRESS:
Uliza Razvodnaya 2; 18 miles (30 km) west of St Petersburg

OPENING HOURS:
Grand Palace: 11 a.m.-6 p.m. (May-October 10.30 a.m.-6 p.m.), Closed Mon and last Tues in the month; Park: 9 a.m.-9 p.m.; Fountains 11 a.m.-5 p.m. (May-October)

GETTING THERE:
Hydrofoil: from Hermitage to Peterhof; Metro: from Baltiyskaya to Peterhof, then bus: 350, 351, 352 or 356

Situated close to the sea and nestling in a magnificent park decorated with golden sculptures, tinkling fountains and dramatic jets of water is the Grand Palace of Peterhof. It forms the heart of the Tsar's family estate and is an impressive property in every respect. Its numerous buildings, sumptuous gardens and famous water features clearly demonstrate their wealth. Strolling through these magnificent grounds today, the visitor gains a sense of the glittering lifestyle enjoyed by Russia's former rulers.

A work of art in the form of an architectural ensemble
Construction work began in 1714 on this breathtaking estate, which Peter the Great intended for use as his summer residence. Situated directly on the Gulf of Finland, approximately 18 miles (30km) from St Petersburg, the

Peterhof Palace is located in a landscaped park covering around 2,471 acres (1,000ha). Several small castles and pavilions are dotted around the estate with the Grand Palace situated on a 65-ft (20-m) high bluff. From here, there are far-reaching views across large areas of this magnificent park. From the North Terrace, the views stretch across a sea channel as far as the Baltic.

The channel not only connects the palace with the sea—the Tsars usually arrived by boat—but it also bisects the Lower Park. The Baroque-style gardens contain over 140 splendid fountains, water features and cascades, for which the Peterhof is renowned. On bright summer days, a sea of flowering plants is visible between the glittering fountains and in the midst of this picturesque setting stands the beautiful palace façade in all its glory.

The gardens took priority
Peter the Great was initially more concerned with landscaping the gardens than with the individual buildings. For the first few years, he contented himself with a modest wooden residence. The architects, Leblond and Braunstein, cultivated numerous areas of woodland and planted avenues of trees. They also planned the first small buildings, such as Monplaisir Castle, built in the Dutch style, of which Peter was so fond. Marly Castle and the Hermitage are situated in the western part of the park.

Construction work on the Grand Palace began in 1714 and lasted until 1725, although it was officially inaugurated as the Tsar's new residence two years before this. The death of Peter the Great in 1725 brought a temporary halt to further plans and it was not until the reign of Tsarina

Elizabeth that the Peterhof was expanded in the mid-18th century. She commissioned the Italian architect Rastrelli to finish the Grand Palace in the Classical style.

A Russian Versailles

Later generations of Romanovs continued to leave their mark on the Peterhof. Nicholas I, for example, had the "Cottage Palace" built in Alexandria Park—an English-style building surrounded by an English-style park. During World War II, the residence was almost completely destroyed. Russian restoration workers invested a great deal of energy and knowledge and brought a meticulous love of detail to bear in restoring it to its original state. Since the 1960s, visitors to Peterhof have been able to admire it in all its glory.

Between 1944 and 1992, the Peterhof was officially known as "Petrodvorez." It is now regarded as the Russian equivalent of Versailles and was designated a World Heritage site in 1990.

In the center of the Peterhof is the Grand Palace with its gleaming façade (above, left).

The magical little Marly Palace was one of the first buildings to be constructed (above).

This Gothic chapel was erected by Nicholas I in Alexandria Park. It is a square building decorated with numerous bronze statues and little turrets (left).

A dream abode

The **GRAND PALACE OF PETERHOF** was the favorite summer residence of an entire dynasty of Tsars

St Petersburg
Russia
Moscow

The Grand Cascade is one of the world's most spectacular fountains—water cascades from the palace terrace over a series of steps into a marble pool (opposite).

Magnificent paintings, ceiling frescoes and gold sculptures decorate the rooms of the palace (below).

Architect Rastrelli extended the Grand Palace and crowned the building with a gilded cupola (bottom right).

Peter the Great had a dream: he wanted to create a residence which stood out from all others on account of its magnificent size, superb architecture, and imposing main building. His answer was to commission the building of the Peterhof, a palace modeled on Versailles, on a site approximately 18 miles (30km) from St Petersburg. The central feature of the palace complex is the "Grand Palace," built between 1714 and 1725.

During the initial phase of the work, a two-story building was created, designed by French architect Jean Baptiste Leblond. On his death, a German architect, Johann Braunstein, took over the task of supervising construction work. Later on, the architects Michetti and Semzov also became involved. Between 1747 and 1752, Tsarina Elizabeth had her favorite architect Rastrelli extended the building to its present dimensions.

Sumptuous additions

The previously simple Baroque-style main building was extended by the addition of two new wings and a further story. Two pavilions were also

added, one of which houses the palace chapel. These additions are decorated with belfries topped with gold cupolas. The middle section is altogether different—it is decorated with a pediment. The three-story façade, measuring 900ft (275m) in length, is finished in shades of yellow, white and gold.

Under Tsarina Elizabeth, the interior of the Grand Palace underwent a complete facelift. Rastrelli began by introducing grandiose furnishings. Some rooms were adorned with gold-trimmed carvings or sumptuous murals and ceiling paintings. Further alterations were carried out during the second half of the 18th century that gave the palace its Classical image.

The Tsar's quarters

Inside the palace, altogether 20 main rooms are currently open to the public. Of these, only one study, the so-called Oak Cabinet, has survived from the days of Peter the Great. The table clock, which is on display in this room, was manufactured around the beginning of the 18th century and is reputed to have belonged to Peter the Great.

Other fascinating exhibits include the shimmering silk carpets and the large paintings of Catherine II and her daughter-in-law, Maria Feodorovna, in the blue guest-room. Visitors can also marvel at the image of Catherine the Great in the vast throne room, which stretches the whole width of the building. A huge painting depicts her holding a drawn sword and wearing the uniform of the Russian Guard. Four more paintings, painted by the English artist Joseph Wright to commemorate the Battle of Chesme, hang opposite the throne, which Peter I had built early in the 18th century.

Several ornate doors lead the way into the Picture Hall, also known as Rotari Hall. Its walls are covered with the portraits of 368 girls, immortalized on canvas by the artist Pietro Rotari. Opulent silk hangings are on display in the Partridge Room—their light blue backgrounds decorated with partridges, garlands of flowers and ears of corn.

Another impressive sight is the white dining room, decorated in shades of cream in strict Classical style. The 18th-century Wedgwood dinner service is always a major attraction.

An abundance of fountains

For over 250 years, 150 fountains, cascades and water jets have operated without the use of pumps: the **PETERHOF FOUNTAINS** represent a masterpiece of technological achievement

The Samson Fountain shoots water 72ft (22m) into the air from the jaws of a golden lion. It forms the central feature of the Grand Cascade built in 1734 (right).

The fountain displays in the midst of a monumental Roman backdrop are another of the Peterhof's main attractions (opposite, top).

Peter the Great planned the cascades, which drop down two levels into a pool and then flow along a channel into the sea (opposite, bottom).

Its abundance of fountains is another reason why the delightful Peterhof estate is often described as "the Russian Versailles." Peter the Great had a weakness for water features and unusual fountains. The system of fountains in the Peterhof gardens represents a unique monument to the Tsar.

Technological masterpiece

The fountain system is a technological masterpiece in itself: Tuvolkov, a hydraulics engineer, constructed a 72-ft (22-m) long pipe system which relies on the natural incline of the landscape and draws water from a high-elevation source without requiring the use of pumps. The system has functioned flawlessly on this principle for almost 300 years. To this day, the 144 fountains and four cascades still depend on this clever system for their water.

One of the most spectacular fountain systems in the world is the Grand Cascade located immediately below the palace—it is flanked by 64 fountains and gilded statues and the water cascades over two steps into a marble pool, whence it flows along a channel into the sea. The Samson Fountain is situated in the central basin. This gilded sculpture entitled "Samson Tearing Open the Jaws of the Lion" was erected in 1734 as a symbol of Russia's victory over Sweden. The lion shoots a 72-ft (22-m) high vertical jet of water from its mouth.

Water-spouting dragon

The Dragon or Chessboard Cascade dating from 1739 is set in a rocky landscape, where water shoots from wild, winged dragons. The Great Mountain Cascade was built at the same time as Marly and features huge lions spouting water that cascades down a series of steps. This fountain system was decorated in 1870 with Italian marble statues. A few years ago, the Lion Cascade below the Hermitage building with its picturesque fountains was also restored to its former glory.

The oldest fountains are the Adam and Eve fountains, positioned at the conjunction of a star-shaped pattern of paths. Other impressive fountains include The Sun Fountain, the Roman Fountain and the Pyramids Fountain. The Dutch garden also features a number of joke fountains, which are guaranteed to surprise visitors as they find themselves sprayed with water. In total, the Peterhof gardens boast 148 marvelously different fountains.

A stroll through Baroque splendor

The **PETERHOF GARDENS** are a combination of Baroque garden design and natural landscape features, and the result is an incomparable whole

The gardens are full of colorful flowerbeds as well as dramatic fountains (opposite, top).

Wonderful avenues lead to the different palaces situated in Peterhof (below).

A gentle breeze wafts from the Gulf of Finland. The summer sun's rays throw soft shadows through the tops of the trees. The path leads straight to a small pavilion where the sound of a splashing fountain delights the ear. The brilliant color provided by flowering shrubs in ornamental flower beds competes with the golden glow of precious sculptures and white marble figures. The senses are well and truly saturated. Anyone taking a stroll through the unique Peterhof Gardens will experience an incomparable landscape of architecture and horticultural mastery.

The gardens were already an all-important feature of Peter the Great's early design plans. He was not merely concerned with erecting a palace, but also with creating an integral work of art based on a combination of architecture and nature as a whole. He therefore provided for not one but several green spaces. Based on the symmetrical concept of Baroque garden design, two large gardens were created: the Lower and the Upper Gardens. Alexandria Park was a later addition. The Lower Garden forms the green area for the numerous water features. A 1,312-ft (400-m) long channel not only links the palace with the sea but also forms the park's central axis.

French Baroque

The French Baroque style is also distinctly evident in the Upper Garden to the north of the palace. Magnificent avenues cross the park, each leading to a specific destination—for example, the Peter and Paul Cathedral, a small pavilion or the palace fountains. At the center of the Upper Garden is the Neptune Fountain with its impressive pool measuring 300 by 108ft (92x33m).

The appearance of the gardens has changed over the years as has the residence complex itself. Following the expansion of the Grand Palace in the 1750s, the park area underwent a corresponding enlargement.

Alexandria Park was not built until the 19th century, when Nicholas I had it created for his wife Alexandra in the English style. Covering an area of 285 acres (115ha), this landscaped park is bordered by the sea in the eastern section of Peterhof. It was stocked in part by plants brought from botanical gardens in St Petersburg and Moscow, and even Hamburg and Marseille. In contrast to the strict geometry of the Baroque gardens, it is possible here to discover unspoilt nature amid the groups of shade-giving trees and sunny glades.

A walk through the Peterhof Gardens reveals a series of fresh, unexpected views for example, of wide—open spaces punctuated with impressive statues (left).

A visit to a fairy-tale land

CATHERINE'S PALACE in **TSARSKOYE SELO**, the most beautiful palace in Russia, has a façade 985ft (300m) long

ADDRESS:
Sadovaya Uliza 7; 15 miles (25km) south of St Petersburg

OPENING TIMES:
Daily 10 a.m.–6 p.m., closed Tues and the last Mon in the month

GETTING THERE:
Metro: From Vitebsky or Moskovskaya to Tsarskoye Selo, then bus: 371 or 382 to Sadovaya Uliza

The impressive façade of Catherine's Palace is one of the architectural highlights of Tsarist Russia. The residence is visited by hundreds of thousands of visitors each year.

No matter how many sumptuous palaces and splendid buildings Russia boasts, the magnificence and treasures of Catherine's Palace in Tsarskoye Selo puts all others in the shade. Situated in the midst of an idyllic landscaped park, the summer residence, with its 985-ft (300-m) façade, houses treasures of inestimable value, including the legendary Amber Room.

When Peter I gave his wife Catherine I the estate at the beginning of the 18th century, no one could have guessed what a cultural jewel would eventually be created here. Catherine's initial instructions were for a smallish stone house to be built and designed by the German architect Johann Braunstein.

A palace memorial to a mother
The palace complex did not achieve its full splendor until 1750, under Elizabeth I, Peter and Catherine's daughter. She had the palace extended by the master of Russian Baroque, Bartolomeo Rastrelli as a memorial to her mother.

Around the main courtyard of the palace, with its magnificent gilded main entrance, are semicircular domestic quarters. The blue and white palace façade is richly decorat-

ed with columns, balustrades and sculptures. The five cupolas of the palace church at the northeastern end of the palace gleam once more in gilded splendor.

The interior of the main salon, designed by Rastrelli and measuring 9,687ft² (900m²), is one of the largest ballrooms in Europe. Ceiling frescoes create a sense of perspective and emphasize the height of the room, while gilt mirrors along the side walls and glittering chandeliers create a breathtaking overall image. The Cavaliers dining hall, in which a luxurious table is laid, is another surviving example of Rastrelli's style.

After 1762, Catherine the Great had many of the rooms renovated by Charles Cameron in the early Classical style and also commissioned new buildings. The Achat pavilion on the south side of the palace, decorated with jasper, marble and lapis lazuli, is regarded as a masterpiece of Classicism. Cameron's Gallery—a temple-style building with tall pillars and Roman sculptures—dates from the same period and houses an exhibition of costumes and uniforms from the 18th and 19th centuries.

In 1811, Tsar Alexander commissioned the addition of an elite school—one of its pupils was Alexander Pushkin. A museum was established there in his honor. In 1937, Tsarskoye Selo was renamed "Pushkin," but its name has now reverted to *Tsarskoye Selo*, which, roughly translated, means "the Tsar's village."

A dazzling wonder

The splendor of the fabled **AMBER ROOM** crowns the luxurious interior of Tsarskoye Selo

Catherine's Palace has always been one of the most sumptuous summer residences, but since 2003 the stream of visitors has increased dramatically. Thousands of people are now flocking to the palace to marvel over a legend—the newly resurrected Amber Room.

The story of the "eighth wonder of the world" began in 1716 when the Prussian king, Friedrich Wilhelm I, made a deal with Tsar Peter I. In return for 55 "Giant Fellows" (*Lange Kerle*) of the Tsar's Guard, Peter the Great received the amber panel decorations for a chamber measuring 183ft^2 (17m^2), which Danish and East Prussian engravers had fashioned for the Soldier King at the beginning of the century.

After Peter's death, this cabinet room was transferred from the summer residence to the Winter Palace before being installed in Catherine's Palace in 1755. Under the direction of Rastrelli, the room was enlarged to include mirrors and inlaid work. By 1770, Catherine the Great was able to impress her guests with a magnificent room measuring 1,076ft^2 (100m^2).

The fabled Amber Room owes its famous reputation not only to its

The Amber Room is the most stunning highlight of Catherine's Palace. The room, which has been restored in minute detail, has sometimes been called the "eighth wonder of the world." Its value is estimated at over 120 million euros.

sumptuous décor, but also to the fact that it went missing in 1945. In the confusion of the final days of the war, it was dismantled and removed to Königsberg Castle, since which time its whereabouts have remained a mystery. Rumors that the treasure was destroyed or sunk in the Baltic Sea have never been verified.

The resurrection

The reconstruction of this mysterious room in Catherine's Palace began in 1979. All that the 50 or so restorers had to help them were some black and white photos taken before the war. The artistically demanding work of cutting and carving was painstakingly carried out in meticulous detail: panels of amber were fashioned into ornamentation, trailing vines and leaves.

In the early 1990s, in the final days before the collapse of the Soviet Union, work had to be halted because of financial difficulties, but by the end of the decade, the fate of the Amber Room had taken a turn for the better.

1.1 tons (1 tonne) of amber, seized from smugglers, was transported from Königsberg to Tsarskoye Selo. A German firm, Deutsche Ruhrgas AG, in Essen also donated 3.5 million euros to the project. When some small original mosaics materialized in Berlin and Bremen, the 20 years of work by Russian restorers were finally vindicated. The new copies are scarcely distinguishable from the original amber. Five hundred thousand individual pieces of "Baltic Gold" were created for the reconstruction.

In May 2003, the reconstructed Amber Room was ceremoniously opened to mark St Petersburg's 300th birthday. This singularly beautiful creation in tones of honey yellow, cherry red, gold and hazelnut brown is just one of the sumptuous interiors to be found in the palace. Many other rooms and salons also boast carvings and sculptures which gleam in golden splendor.

Elegant English landscaping

The imaginative beauty of the extensive parkland around Tsarskoye Selo rivals the sumptuous palace

St Petersburg
Russia
Moscow

The park surrounding Catherine's Palace is as great an attraction as the building. The flowerbeds are laid out in a strict symmetrical pattern (right).

The garden features have been designed in meticulous detail. The wrought-iron work of the main gate is particularly impressive (above).

The small bathing-house nestles romantically in the upper garden (top right).

Small pavilions and attractive sculptures are harmoniously integrated into the landscape.

If you have been dazzled by the glittering splendor of the Amber Room, the extensive parkland around Tsarskoye Selo provides an opportunity for relaxation and a chance to rest the eye and the spirit.

The so-called French Garden was commissioned by Elizabeth I in the mid-18th century and is based on a symmetrical design whereby topiary features and areas of gravel and slate are laid out to an overall geometrical design. The charming pavilion, known as the "grotto," situated on the shores of a small lake, was built at the same time.

Raised dining tables

The main path through the French Gardens leads to the Hermitage, built by Rastrelli between 1744 and 1756. A special feature of this pavilion was that after a meal the large dining tables could be raised up to ceiling height so that the dining salon could be transformed into a ballroom.

In 1770, Catherine the Great took her plans for redesigning the park-

land and grounds a stage further. She engaged John Bush, the son-in-law of Charles Cameron, as her garden architect and commissioned him to create an English-style garden around the large existing pond. Its extensive grassy areas, bridges, mounds and winding paths create a natural and romantic atmosphere.

Despite its orientation toward nature, Catherine Park is generously endowed with monuments which the Tsarina had erected for every victory in the Russo-Turkish War (1768–1774).

The last Tsar's house

On the occasion of the wedding of her favorite nephew, the future Alexander I, Catherine presented him with a palace within the Tsarskoye Selo park grounds. Alexander Palace, an elegant building in the Classical style, was constructed in 1792 and named after him. It was to become the main residence of the last generation of tsars. In 1917, Nicholas II and his family were interned here before being taken to Ekaterinburg and murdered.

The palace is surrounded by Alexander Park, an area of wonderful wilderness that was used for hunting. A Chinese village with a theater and a Gothic Revival chapel are harmoniously integrated into the landscape.

A Tsarina's love nest

GATCHINA Palace was a truly royal gift for Catherine to give to her lover, Count Orlov

LOCATION:
28 miles (45km) south of St Petersburg; St Petersburg oblast

SIZE:
Approximately 80,000 inhabitants

GETTING THERE:
Via motorway or rail (from Baltiyskaya Metro station) toward Pskov

SPECIAL FEATURES:
Between 1923 to 1929, the town was renamed Trozk after the revolutionary, Trotzky.

Count Grigory Orlov was the love of Catherine the Great's life. Catherine is reputed to have had over 20 different lovers, but the Tsarina probably only really loved a few of them. Count Orlov was one of these—and her feelings were based on more than just the fact that he helped her to murder her husband Peter III. The extensive correspondence between the two of them is an established fact, as are two spectacular gifts: Orlov presented his lover with some extremely valuable diamonds, named after himself, which were later used to grace the sovereign's scepter. Catherine in turn gave him Gatchina Palace as a gift.

The palace, which is situated in the midst of an extensive landscaped park, lies 28 miles (45km) southwest of St Petersburg. It was constructed between 1766 and 1781 by architect Antonio Rinaldi, who designed a three-story structure with pentagonal towers in the early Russian-Classical style.

Gatchina Palace was a gift from Catherine the Great to her lover, Count Orlov. It was later extended to encompass 900 rooms (opposite).

The Palace boasts a beautiful landscape park, which includes several small, very picturesque buildings (lower left).

Walks through the park frequently reveal stunning views; for example, of this church (left).

The broad pathways provide many opportunities for walking (below).

It was not its exterior that made the palace famous, but its sumptuous interior that became renowned throughout Europe. In keeping with its role as an intimate trysting-place for the Tsarina and her favorite, the palace was decorated with erotic murals and elegant furniture.

The extensive park, with its White Lake and Black Lake, its small pavilions, bridges and islands and its idyllic natural appearance, is regarded by many as the first Russian landscape park.

Extended to encompass 900 rooms

Following Orlov's death, the estate passed into the hands of Catherine's son, the future Tsar Paul I, who had architect Vincenzo Brenna convert it during the 1790s into a fortress-like palace complex. During the process, the intimate paintings were removed. The palace was fortified with bastions and ditches while the building was extended to contain 900 rooms. Thereafter, it functioned both as a summer residence and as an arena for military exercises and parades.

After the assassination of Paul I in 1801, the estate was not used again until 50 years later when the Tsar and his family began using it as a hunting lodge. In 1881, Alexander III went so far as to make the palace, which by then had been faced in gray limestone and was heavily secured, his main residence. His reason for this was his fear of being murdered in St Petersburg or Moscow.

Under the German occupation during World War II, the palace was completely devastated and the park laid waste as a result of a fire. Even to this day, it is not fully restored, but the visitor can nevertheless admire some magnificent rooms, including the marble dining room and the White Hall decorated in the style of Catherine's era.

The influence of 18th-century English and French styles on the park landscape with its lake features is very much in evidence. Some of the bridges and pavilions remain in a dilapidated state, but many of the buildings have been restored.

On the shores of the Black Lake is the Priory Palace of Nikolay Lvov, who created a knight's castle from pressed earth.

A delightful Venus Pavilion stands on the Isle of Love, providing magical views of the surrounding area, the Eagle Pavilion and the little birch house, which from the outside appears to be a simple wooden hut, but is lavishly furnished on the inside with reflecting mirrors and exquisite wood carvings.

Competing with the Tsar

Prince Menshikov was trying to rival Peter the Great when he built Oranienbaum Palace

LOCATION:
18 miles (30km) west of St Petersburg on the shores of the Baltic; St Petersburg oblast

SIZE:
Approximately 45,000 inhabitants

GETTING THERE:
By rail from Baltiyskaya Metro station or by bus from Avtovo Metro station: 300 and 424-A

SPECIAL FEATURES:
The place was renamed Lomonosov in 1945 after Mikhail Vassilyevich Lomonosov, a Russian poet, scientist, and reformer of the Russian language.

One of the aspects that govern friendships between men is that they work best if they are based on an equal footing. This was no less true of the legendary friendship between Prince Alexander Menshikov and Peter the Great. The enormously wealthy prince, who was famed for his lavish lifestyle, was tired of always being overshadowed by his chess and drinking partner. He became consumed with the idea of owning a more grandiose residence than the Tsar. The result was Oranienbaum, one of Russia's most impressive palaces.

In 1710, Menshikov commissioned his two favorite architects, Giovanni Maria Fontana and Gottfried Saebel, to build a new palace on a site covering approximately 1,186 acres (480ha) situated 25 miles (40km) west of St Petersburg.

His vision became a reality: work on the feudal mansion was completed in 1725 and the finished building bore a very strong resemblance to the future Peterhof. Menshikov was now the proud owner of a dazzling two-story building situated adjacent to the town of the same name and complete with towers, a corona and arched galleries ending in octagonal pavilions topped with mighty domes. The sumptuous building derived its name from the orangeries which formed part of the palace and park complex.

Friendships cannot be inherited, however, and Prince Menshikov was to discover this to his cost. His enjoyment of the picturesque idyll of his estate on the Gulf of Finland was short-lived. After the Tsar's death, he fell out of favor and was banished to Siberia by Peter's daughter.

A parade ground

Oranienbaum now found itself in the hands of the sovereign, who turned it into another summer residence. It was enlarged even further during the reigns of Peter III and Catherine the Great.

Between 1758 and 1762, Antonio Rinaldi built the military-minded Tsar a fortified settlement in the shape of a 12-pronged star. The delightful gate and a small castle of Petrstadt Fortress are the only buildings to have survived from this period. The castle was a simple structure with a large chamber, a cabinet and a bedroom with Chinese lacquer painting.

Catherine the Great was very fond of Eastern culture. In 1768, Rinaldi

The Sledding Hill Pavilion was particularly popular with the nobility. Extensive restoration work has now restored it to its former splendor (left).

In its day, the Chinese Palace was a small architectural sensation (below, left).

The residence itself was encircled by a large wall (below).

built her a Chinese Palace, a richly decorated pleasure palace, furnished on a predominantly Oriental theme. In those days, there was a tendency for Russians to refer to any exotic style as "Chinese."

The most splendid room in the new building was the Glass Bead Room, for which the builders used colored glass manufactured by Mikhail Lomonosov, a university academic. He was honored in 1945 when the nearby settlement was renamed after him.

Another small pavilion known as Sledding Hill was built between 1762 and 1777. This small palace acquired its unusual name from one of the favourite pursuits of the nobility—winter sledding down the hill on which the pavilion was built.

Situated between the hill and the Chinese Palais is the Upper Park with its stock of fascinating old trees. The Lower Park extends behind the Grand Palace. Despite all the extravagant splendor of the buildings, which Catherine the Great had built in Oranienbaum, she is reputed to have spent no more than 48 hours there.

The capital city's guard

For a long time, this prohibited area was just a mark on the map, but **KRONSTADT** is once more open to visitors

LOCATION:
18 miles (30km) north-west of St Petersburg on the Baltic island of Kotlin in the Gulf of Finland; St Petersburg oblast

SIZE:
Approximately 50,000 inhabitants

GETTING THERE:
By communal taxi from Chernaya Rechka Metro station

The fact that Kronstadt's sailors have mutiny in their blood was something that Tsar Nicholas II discovered to his cost. They were involved in the 1905 uprising against the country's autocratic ruler and went on to support the Bolsheviks in the October Revolution. They also rebelled against their new rulers in 1921, an uprising which Lenin quashed in a brutal and bloody manner.

Since Peter's new capital was not situated on the Baltic, Kronstadt assumed the role of port. Mighty fortifications, which were still being enlarged right up until the 19th century, were designed to keep enemies at bay. Kronstadt quickly developed into the main naval training center for the Imperial Navy. Important research institutes were also established here. During World War II, Kronstadt suffered even more than Leningrad under the German blockade, but the German Wehrmacht found the heavily fortified base too difficult to overcome.

Tsarist naval fortress
Kronstadt was established during the reign of Peter the Great on the Kotlin peninsula in the Gulf of Finland as a naval fortress with dockyard facilities. Throughout the Communist era, it was the most securely protected naval base for the Baltic Fleet, a fact that turned it into a closed town. Until November 1996, when the Army handed the city's administration back into civilian hands, Kronstadt remained a spot on the map as far as the inhabitants of St Petersburg, barely 18 miles (30km) away, were concerned.

They were amazed to discover that this town of around 40,000 inhabitants with its arrow-straight, broad avenues and generously pro-

portioned squares was very similar to their own St Petersburg. This is hardly surprising considering that it was founded just one year after its sister town. It was laid out to a regular ground-plan and is similarly characterized by long avenues and numerous green spaces.

St Nicholas Naval Cathedral

The city's most distinctive landmark is the St Nicholas Naval Cathedral, which was completed in 1913 and can be seen from a considerable distance. The barracks, naval depots and stores, designed by Mikhail Vetoshnikov between 1785 and 1796, are sadly in a very poor state of repair.

Since the army's withdrawal from Kronstadt, the living standards of its residents have deteriorated dramatically. For this reason, many people commute daily to St Petersburg in order to earn a living.

For many years, Kronstadt was a restricted military zone and remained closed to visitors. St Nicholas Naval Cathedral, with its mighty dome, remains particularly well preserved (above and left).

In tune with nature

PAVLOVSK Park is one of the most beautiful of its kind in Europe

LOCATION:
18 miles (30km) south of St Petersburg

SIZE:
Approximately 17,000 inhabitants

GETTING THERE:
By rail from Vitebsky Station

Catherine the Great bestowed a truly royal gift upon her son Paul I and his wife, Maria Feodorovna, on the birth of her first grandchild—the estate of Pavlovsk, 18 miles (30km) south of St Petersburg.

In 1782 construction began on a sumptuous palace and its 1,482 acres (600ha) of land which were destined to become one of the most beautiful landscape parks in Europe. Over the course of time, a town of the same name grew up around the residence.

The work of a Scotsman

Charles Cameron, a Scotsman, began construction of the three-story Classical-style palace, to which Vincenzo Brenna later added galleries and wings. Architects Voronikhin and Rossi were also involved in its interior design during the early 19th century. Maria Feodorovna, a Wurttemberg princess, declared Pavlovsk to be her favorite residence. She turned this sumptuous palace into a temple of the muses and organized literary readings by famous writers.

The interior of this magnificent building, which was destroyed during World War II, has been completely restored and now forms a magical backdrop for special occasions. The large, horseshoe-shaped throne room alone measures 4,305ft² (400m²) and was decorated with lavish ceiling frescoes by the Italian painter Pietro Gonzaga. The Greek Hall is designed to resemble a temple with green marble pillars and statues. The circular

Italian Hall with its domed roof boasts a chandelier made of crystal peacock's feathers.

An Egyptian vestibule and the Halls of Peace and War, decorated in lavish Rococo style and featuring scenes from the Trojan War, are the main showpieces of the palace. Many items of furniture, which were removed to safety at the outbreak of war, have now been returned to their original positions for the visitor to admire.

A garden for art

If the palace is a poem of architecture, then the park which surrounds Pavlovsk must be a dream come true. It was created for Maria Feodorovna in 1803 and was largely the work of Italian stage set designer and garden designer Pietro Gonzaga. He was engaged in the project for 25 years, during which time every artist involved in the building of the palace also left his mark on the landscaped park.

The estate park, which follows the small Slavyanka River valley through rolling countryside, gives the impression of being entirely natural despite having been created using all the skills of English-style garden design. Finnish oaks, linden trees from Lübeck and flowers from Holland

and England all found a place here. Lakes, numerous sculptures, 18 pavilions and 12 bridges were integrated harmoniously into the landscape, turning a walk into a romantic journey of discovery.

Leafy glades

The little "Milk House," built by Cameron in 1782, resembles a Swiss chalet, yet it is furnished with gilded furniture. A sculpture of the "Three Graces," fashioned from a single piece of marble, is surrounded by 16 Ionic columns. The Tsar's wife had a favorite spot: the "Rose Pavilion" created by Voronikhin in 1811. Other idyllic places include the "Temple of Friendship" with its Doric columns and Maria Feodorovna's "Monument for the Parents."

This magical park reveals unexpected views at almost every turn. This is one of the reasons why Pavlovsk in the mid-19th century became one of the most popular destinations for St Petersburg society. To facilitate travel, the first Russian railway was built between St Petersburg and Pavlovsk linking the two towns. It was built by the English firm of "Vauxhall," from which derives the Russian word "voksal," meaning "railway."

Pavlovsk Park is regarded as one of the most beautiful in Europe and it is possible to wander for hours while enjoying the different seasons (above).

The sculptures are mainly located close to the Palace (opposite).

The Palace was a gift from Catherine the Great to her son Paul to mark the birth of her first grandson (left).

Wooden marvels

The churches on the island of **KIZHI POGOST** are fine examples of carpentry craftsmanship

LOCATION:
Kizhi Island in Lake Onega, northeast of Petrozavodsk

OPENING TIMES:
Daily until dusk between May and September

GETTING THERE:
By hydrofoil from Petrozavodsk between May and September

The excursion steamer cuts majestically through the shimmering blue waters of Lake Onega. Pink bands of light on the horizon signal the dawn of the day while the dark silhouette of Southern Karelia's "marvel in wood" situated on Kizhi, a narrow island roughly 12 miles (20km) in length, is only just distinguishable.

In the blue haze of daylight, the fascinating diversity of features in the Church of the Transfiguration of Christ, which dates from 1714, give it the appearance of an unearthly masterpiece.

Protection from the Tatars

The densely wooded area around the lake has, since the 14th century, provided shelter to those seeking refuge from invading Tatar hordes. This gave rise to a settlement of farms and villages, the ecclesiastical center of which was the island of Kizhi Pogost.

During the 18th century, two remarkable wooden structures were constructed here. They were produced without the aid of any designs or sketches and created purely "by eye" on the part of the master builders. Together with a high bell tower, they form a remarkable group.

The nine-domed Protection of the Virgin Church was a winter church, capable of being heated. The building, topped by an 88-ft (27-m) tall central dome and eight additional cupolas, is modeled on the simple architecture of a Russian farmhouse. The builders added three further rooms to its basic floor plan and the lobby, refectory and public room are lit by numerous windows.

The design of the church is impressive, if somewhat imbalanced as it stands adjacent to the perfectly proportioned Church of the Transfiguration of the Savior, which was used as a summer church. It bears distinct similarity with St Basil's Cathedral in Moscow—the astonishing structure is crowned with 22 cupolas. Nestor, the builder in charge of its construction, was so overcome by his own masterpiece that he is said to have thrown his axe into the middle of Lake Onega, saying: "There never was and there never will be another church like this."

Forgotten techniques

Since the 1960s, the island of Kizhi Pogost, to the northwest of St Petersburg, has also been home to an exhibition of unique wooden architecture, which consists of around 60 exhibits taken from various regions and reconstructed on this site. Farmhouses and windmills, bath houses and granaries, forges and chapels have been relocated in their new island home and constitute a spectacular ensemble.

The little Lazarus Church came originally from Murom Monastery on Lake Ladoga. Built around 1390, it is thought to be the oldest Russian wooden church.

Since so little survives of ancient carpentry techniques, Russia depends on foreign aid to maintain these architectural monuments. It is a matter of international concern to preserve this cultural heritage site in the far North.

The builders constructed their wooden churches purely by eye without the aid of plans. The Church of the Transfiguration is regarded as Russia's most beautiful wooden church, flanked on its right by the Protection of the Virgin Church (above, right).

The 22 domes constitute a confection of onion domes—they also prevent the snow from settling on the roof (adjacent).

A wooden protective wall topped with wooden slats surrounds the ensemble (center).

A tower, topped with a conical roof, adjacent to the familiar onion-shaped dome, is a distinctive feature of the reconstructed St Michael's Chapel (below, right).

On the White Sea, a new start

Once a citadel of the Orthodox religion, Solovetsky Monastery later became a prison. It is now a UNESCO World Heritage site

LOCATION:
In the northeast of Karelia at the mouth of the Onega estuary where it discharges into the White Sea

OPENING TIMES:
Daily from May to September until dusk

GETTING THERE:
By plane or ship from Arkhangelsk

The massive monastery walls are 42ft (13m) high and have eight towers (right).

One of the monastery's bells once again calls the monks to prayer (opposite).

No nation is fonder of bestowing nicknames than the Russians and the inhabitants of Solovetsky affectionately refer to their lonely island in the White Sea as "Solovki."

The island's 1,300 residents, who voluntarily moved to this remote island near the Polar circle after World War II, chose, of all things, an elephant as their symbol. "*Slon,*" the inscription on a weathered plaque on a wooden house in the main settlement, is indeed the Russian word for "elephant." Choosing this thick-skinned beast as their insignia reflects the Russians' black sense of humor.

In the language of the NKWD secret service, the main instrument of the Stalinist reign of terror "People's Office for the Interior," the abbreviation "SLON" simply means "Solovetsky Camp for Special Purposes."

In 1923, CPSU General Secretary Stalin had the old buildings in Solovetsky Monastery converted into the Soviet Union's first Gulag. Up until 1939, this prototype death camp served as a place to which tens of

After the October Revolution, Solovetsky Monastery, with its 22ft (7m) thick walls, served as a forced labor camp (opposite).

The Constantine Chapel, built atop a hill, was designed in the Classical style (left).

thousands of real and supposed opponents of the regime were exiled. Later, it became a forced labor camp.

No matter how dreadful its recent history, however, its cultural and historical significance cannot be dismissed. Around 1430, hermits built a retreat in this godforsaken part of northern Karelia on the main island in the western part of the White Sea. It marked the northernmost outpost of the Orthodox faith.

Outpost in the far north

A century after the original retreat was first established, the monastery began to grow in importance. By dint of much hard work, the monks built roads and linked lakes by means of channels to ensure drinking water supplies. Some factories produced ceramics as well as bricks, with which they built the mighty Ascension Church, the refectory and the monk's cells.

Thanks to the fortifications finished in 1594, the actual monastery and domestic quarters remained securely protected over an area of 12 aces (5ha). The monastery is encircled by granite walls up to 22ft (7m) thick and 36ft (11m) wide and features a main pentagonal tower together with seven further towers. In 1615, workshops were established behind these walls producing icons, sculptures, ceramics, and artworks

that were prized throughout the empire. Tanners, tailors and shoemakers worked in the cellars taking care of the needs of the residents. By 1660, around 50 saltworks were created outside the monastery and several smelting ovens kept pace with the demand for metal.

With its sophisticated harbor and dry dock, Solovetsky Monastery not only served ambitious Russian towns as a reliable commercial center but also became a center of pilgrimage.

The 1917 Revolution marked the end of the monks' community. One of the Red Guards' first actions after seizing power was to close down the hydro-power station, completed in 1912 and drive out the monks. The various infrastructures and the monastery itself fell into neglect.

Following the monks' return, the community has tried to resurrect the old craft skills and technical traditions. The Nobel Prize winner for Literature, Alexander Solzhenitsyn, donated a fish cutter and Moscow gave its assurance that foreigners would not be allowed to acquire property on the island. A museum on the island serves as a reminder of this dark period in its history.

Scandinavian charm

VYBORG, the pearl of Karelia, boasts a remarkable architectural legacy from Scandinavian times

LOCATION:
Karelia lies in north-west Russia in the Leningrad region

BEST TIME TO VISIT:
Between May and September

GETTING THERE:
Rail links from Helsinki and St Petersburg

It is no accident that Friedrich Wilhelm Murnau's silent film classic *Nosferatu* shows Count Dracula's ship docking in the fog-covered port of "Wisborg." Depending on weather conditions, this small town in the far north can appear either attractive and peaceful or dark and mysterious.

Vyborg, known as *Viipuri* in Finnish, is a remote and lonely place situated in the Finnish Lakeland. Vyborg's very appearance distinguishes it from other Old Russian towns in the surrounding area—the reason being that it has been built in the Scandinavian Style.

Long history of defense
The town now numbers 78,000 inhabitants and has a long history of defending itself. From the 13th century on, it served the Swedes as a bastion against the Teutonic Knights and the Russian troops of the legendary Alexander Nevsky of Novgorod. For

almost 500 years, it found itself repeatedly under siege—though never vanquished—until it was annexed in 1710 by Admiral Count Apraxin and ceded to the Russian Empire.

Already an important trading town in the Middle Ages, it flourished even more spectacularly in the 19th century as a result of the construction of the Saimaa Canal, which linked the Finnish Lakeland to the Baltic.

The port was especially significant. Later, an iron smelting plant was also established here and Vyborg became a center of machine engineering.

Connected to the rest of the world
The railway line from Helsinki to St Petersburg also helped to connect the town to the rest of the world. The town and its 18,000 inhabitants already boasted six churches, a Goth-

ic palace, a college and a navigation school. After World War I, the former Duchy of Finland threw off the Russian yoke and Vyborg became Finnish. With 80,000 inhabitants, it was at that time the second biggest town in the country. After it was recaptured by the Red Army however, all the Swedes, Finns and Germans living there were forced to leave.

"Fat Catherine"

Nowadays, the only reminders of this era are some surviving architectural features. The castle, constructed in 1293, is now a museum that illustrates the history of the region. From St Olaf's Tower there are spectacular views over the town. One of the remaining features of the old 16th-century fortifications is the "Fat Catherine." This round tower, situated in the marketplace, has now been converted into a restaurant and is a popular meeting-place for young and old.

The bells in the Clock Tower, completed in 1490, were a gift from Tsarina Catherine II. The old houses from the Finnish era are picturesque and it is true to say that Vyborg has managed to retain a certain Scandinavian appeal.

Situated between the Gulf of Finland and Lake Ladoga, Vyborg's most famous landmark is its Gothic castle (above).

Vyborg's castle played an important part in Murnau's film *Nosferatu* (below, left).

These residences were built toward the end of the 19th century and symbolize Vyborg's economic power (left).

An island monastery

Covering over 6,950 square miles (18,000km²), Lake Ladoga is Europe's largest inland lake

LOCATION:
Northwest Russia, Leningrad region

OPENING TIMES:
Daily until dusk from May to September

GETTING THERE:
By train and ship from St Petersburg

Lightning splits the heavily overcast sky; at any moment it seems as if waves might capsize the boat with the three men on board as it plows through the churning waters. With his left hand, the man with the moustache holds firmly onto the wheel while signaling with his right hand to his two companions, cowering fearfully in the vessel, to row harder.

This is the scene in an 1820 oil painting by K. K. Stein, which depicts a particularly dangerous trip across Lake Ladoga. Close observation of the helmsman reveals an unmistakable resemblance to Tsar Peter I, a savior in the hour of greatest need.

Covering an expanse of over 6,950 miles² (18,000km²), Lake Ladoga, in southern Karelia, not far from the Finnish border, is Europe's largest inland sea. Running from north to south, it measures just over 136 miles

(220km) in length and 50 miles (80km) at its widest point.

Until 1809 the lake was owned by Sweden, but when Finland was ceded to the Tsar's empire the northwestern part of the lake became part of Russia. In 1940, at the end of the Soviet-Finnish Winter War, the entire lake became part of the Soviet Union.

Schlüsselburg Fortress
After about six hours of traveling upriver along the Neva, one reaches a monument of special historic significance, which played an important role in Swedish-Russian relations—the Schlüsselburg Fortress on Orekhov island, which Peter I captured from Sweden in 1702. It was subsequently used as a place of exile. During World War II, Schlüsselburg Fortress suffered major damage and has since fallen into ruins.

Valaam

Valaam is one of the largest rocky islands in Lake Ladoga and the site of an important monastery. It is very popular as a place of pilgrimage and the monastery church with its golden cupolas is a reminder of the days when the monastery was home to large communities of monks. Since 1998, three of the five monastic retreats have been reoccupied by monks.

A path through the cloister leads to Mount Sion, beneath which a retreat known as the Gethsemane Retreat has been built in the forest. The monks have meanwhile crowned Mount Eleon with the Ascension Chapel, with its striking turquoise roof. Natural beauty and the legacy of human creativity have combined to produce a unique atmosphere on Valaam, which was once a magnet for writers and composers.

Novaya Ladoga

Situated at the point where the Volkhov river flows into Lake Ladoga is another gem: Novaya Ladoga, one of Russia's oldest towns. In its present form, the town dates back to the 17th century. Its wooden houses, decorated with carvings, are some of the most outstanding examples of their kind in Russia and are being gradually restored.

A silver gate to heaven

In the 16th century, the Abbot of **KIRILLOV BELOZERSKY** Monastery was Russia's biggest landowner

LOCATION:
On the shores of Lake Siverskoye in the Vologda region

OPENING TIMES:
Daily until dusk from May to September

GETTING THERE:
Bus connections from Vologda

No sooner had the master spoken than his pupil immediately put his wise words into practice. Toward the end of the 14th century, Kirill of Belozero, a noble lord, following the advice of his teacher, Sergius of Radonez, journeyed to Lake Siverskoye in northern Russia where he built a small shelter, followed by a wooden Ascension Chapel.

When other monks began to join him, further living quarters were constructed, thus marking the birth of one of the region's most important monasteries. In their conflict with the Principality of Novgorod, the Muscovite rulers regarded it as a strategic point for trade with the north.

Even in the 16th century, the monastery, which was significantly influenced by the model of the Trinity Monastery near Moscow, was already an extremely rich landowner. Ivan the Terrible, who was an occasional visitor, even had his own cell in the cloister.

In later centuries, undesirables were frequently banished behind Kirillov Belozersky's great walls, which measured 2,400ft (732m) in length and were 23ft (7m) thick.

Russia's greatest abbey church

The monastery is comprised of two separate priories with 11 churches, most of which date from the 16th century. The Assumption Cathedral, which was built in 1497 by the master builders of Rostov-Veliki, was Russia's largest abbey church. Its iconostasis features numerous ancient icons, arranged in five tiers above a massive silver heaven's gate, a masterpiece which Tsar Alexis gave to the monastery in 1645.

The oldest church in the second priory was dedicated to St John the Precursor and commissioned by the father of Ivan the Terrible soon after his visit in 1528. In subsequent years, however, the monks incurred the

Tsar's displeasure when they constructed St Vladimir's Chapel over the tomb of Prince Vorotynsky, who had been banished there in exile. It became Russia's first family mausoleum.

The monastery defense walls, which feature numerous towers, were built by a French architect. After the Soviets secularized the monastery, it was turned into a museum. It includes a special room containing an exhibition of items of ancient craftsmanship. A large part of the monastery still serves as a museum of history, art and architecture.

Surrounded by fortified walls, the monastery consists of two priories with 11 churches (above).

After the monastery complex was nationalized, it was turned into a museum in 1924. The monastery library and other precious treasures were moved to Moscow or St Petersburg. It was not until 1998 that the monks were allowed to return (left).

A gift from St Nilus

Founded by a hermit on an island in Lake Seliger, Nilov Monastery is a historical landmark

LOCATION:
Lake Seliger is situated in the Tver region

OPENING TIMES:
Daily until dusk from May to September

GETTING THERE:
By boat from Ostashkov

Toward the end of the 16th century, Nilus, who was later canonized, was searching for a suitably secluded spot when he came across a remote island in a lake now known as Lake Seliger. The place was not entirely unknown even then: the island, now known as Stolbny, had already played an earlier role in the history of the Christianization of the north. Two of its earlier inhabitants, the monks Ostashko and Temofey, had left the island long before and moved to the mainland where they founded the town of Ostashkov, a settlement which has retained much of its Old Russian charm to this day.

Led by Nilus, a monastery complex gradually developed, which was later remodeled along neoclassical lines. It is one of the largest of its kind in this part of Europe. Some of the churches were built in the 17th century and in 1812 an elegant quayside was added. The large monastery cathedral was completed in 1825 after 40 years of construction. By the outbreak of the October Revolution, up to 40,000 pilgrims a year were visiting the site.

When Moscow's Patriarch Tikhon visited a year later, the Nilski Monastir was no longer a cloister. It was rumored that the priest had brought Anastasia, the young Romanov princess. She was said to be the only member of the Tsar's family to have escaped execution in Ekaterinburg. Tikhon is said to have hidden her in a room beneath the main cathedral. What is truth and what is fiction will probably never be discovered.

One thing we do know for sure is that the Patriarch, who had always had a fascination for music, immediately ordered a special building to be built for the monastery's musicians. They devoted themselves to religious music and lived in the cloister with their families.

The island came to the notice of other musicians, who decided to move there, and it was not long before a new direction began to emerge, which combined religious elements with a swing towards traditional folk music and jazz, a style of music, newly popular in the country.

Stalin's decision to turn this remote island into a camp for Polish prisoners marked the beginning of a dark chapter in the island's history. Several architectural monuments were destroyed during this period. After the internees were transferred to Kalinin, formerly known as Tver, the camp gradually fell into decline. It is thanks to a group of musicians from Leningrad (present-day St Petersburg) that the Nilov monastery was reoccupied in 1948 and partly restored. They founded the Tikhon music collective and breathed fresh life into the monastery.

Nilov Monastery is especially famous for its neoclassical architecture. Some of its churches date from the 17th century (lower left).

The monastery's cathedral was built between 1821 and 1825 (lower right).

During the summer months, excursion boats take visitors to Stolbny Island in Lake Seliger (left).

Many of the monastery's sacred buildings, including this chapel, which were destroyed after 1917, have been commendably restored (below).

Begun anew

The modern city of **KALININGRAD** replaced the old town of Königsberg in 1946

LOCATION:
In the Russian part of East Prussia's Kaliningrad region

BEST TIME TO VISIT:
Between May and September

GETTING THERE:
Direct flights to Kaliningrad from several west European airports

The city's most famous son is undoubtedly Immanuel Kant, a philosopher of the Enlightenment, whose boast at the end of his life was that he had never left Königsberg. He was laid to rest in his beloved hometown on a river island named after him. His tomb is situated behind the cathedral, one of the few surviving old buildings of this once flourishing trading center on the Pregolya River. A statue of the philosopher, completed in the mid-19th century, went missing in 1945, but has since been replaced with a copy that now stands outside the university.

Economic prosperity after 1871

First established in the middle of the 13th century, this capital city of East Prussia experienced its most significant economic boom after 1871, following the founding of the German Empire. The East European Fair was regularly held here from 1920 onward and it was here that Germany's first civil aviation airport was sited.

As one of leading cities in the beleaguered Third Reich, it had already suffered serious damage as a result of bombing raids in 1944. It was captured by the Red Army on April 9th. The historic center of the

town, comprising the Altstadt, Löbenicht and Kneiphof districts, was systematically destroyed. Nothing was to be left that could serve as a reminder of its former inhabitants, who, almost without exception, had been expelled westward.

Parks and squares in the city center

After 1946, the town, which was largely repopulated with citizens from all over the Soviet Union, was renamed after the Stalinist politician, Mikhail Kalinin.

To this day, Moscow refuses permission for the town to revert to its original name. There are historical, ideological and political reasons for this. Modern-day Kaliningrad, as one of the great cooperative projects of the Soviet veterans, was intended to usher in a new epoch. Instead of buildings, a city center was created which consisted of parks, squares and broad parade avenues.

Some 19th-century historic buildings have been reconstructed, however, including the old stock exchange. The cathedral, which was restored with German aid, is now a cultural center.

Kaliningrad is the main town in the administrative region of the same name, an enclave surrounded by Lithuania and Poland, which includes the annexed southern part of Eastern Prussia.

Russia's most western town, Kaliningrad is home to one of the country's most important universities and is regarded as a significant cultural center. Its inhabitants, however, continue to suffer severely as a consequence of chronic economic problems.

Following extensive renovation work, Kaliningrad Cathedral on Kant Island is now a cultural center (left, opposite).

The completion of the Orthodox Cathedral of Christ the Savior in the center of Kaliningrad marked the town's 750th anniversary (left).

As Russia's most westerly city with access to the Baltic, Kaliningrad is still an important port (left, opposite).

Magnificent villas in the suburbs bear testimony to the city's early economic prosperity (below).

Cradle of culture

NOVGOROD can look back on its long history and rich traditions with pride and self-assurance

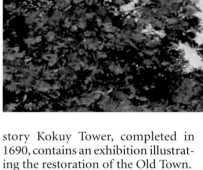

LOCATION:
2½ hours by car southeast of St Petersburg; where the River Oka joins the Volga; Nizhny Novgorod oblast

SIZE:
Approximately 1.4 million inhabitants

GETTING THERE:
By bus or car; organized excursions from St Petersburg

SPECIAL FEATURES:
Novgorod has long been regarded by art enthusiasts as Russia's architectural Mecca

The citizens of Novgorod were never lacking in self-confidence. As far back as 1136, the townsfolk, who called their city *Gospodin Velikiy Novgorod* (Lord Novgorod the Great), had dismissed their princely ruler, accusing him of having abused his official duties.

Even before this putsch in Old Russia, Novgorod merchants had succeeded in limiting the prince's power to representative and military functions. After his dismissal from office, the popular assembly, known as the Veche, assumed complete ruling power.

Power in the hands of the Council

From that time onward, the members of the urban "Council," as Novgorod's governing body was known, were determined by the Veche. From 1433, this illustrious council convened in the Gothic vaulted chambers of the Facetted Palace. These chambers, which once witnessed ceremonial receptions and court proceedings, now house an exhibition of ancient items of craftsmanship.

For almost 350 years, the people's parliament controlled the fate of this northern Hanseatic trading town, which extended over an area of 370 acres (150ha) and was unusually large by any standards.

During Novgorod's time of greatest prosperity, the town's merchants, who had the reputation of being distinctly adventurous, expanded their sphere of influence from the Baltic coasts to the Urals and the Arctic Ocean. Merchants' guilds gave generous donations for the construction of churches, including the clifftop Church of St John the Baptist, completed in 1130.

"Where there is St Sophia, there is Novgorod" is a well-known saying in a city where the oldest historical building is the Cathedral of St Sophia in the kremlin (1045–1062). Begun just a few years after the completion of the Kiev church by the same name, its Novgorod namesake—a five-domed cruciform basilica with three apses—turned out to be just as magnificent as its Kiev predecessor.

The Novgorod School

The Church of Theodor Stratilates on the Brook, built around 1360, is an outstanding example of Novgorod's unique style of church architecture in the 14th century. During the same period, the "Novgorod School," which had emerged in the 12th century, was producing some of its greatest works under the influence of icon painter Theophanes the Greek. Thanks to its school of painting, the leading town in the "Novgorod Empire" became known as Old Russia's "cradle of culture."

The town was eventually annexed by Moscow. The kremlin's several-story Kokuy Tower, completed in 1690, contains an exhibition illustrating the restoration of the Old Town.

Master builders from Yaroslavl erected the five-domed Church of the Annunciation, completed in 1688 in traditional Volga style and featuring galleries, magnificent window surrounds and a wealth of ceramic ornamentation. Tsarina Catherine II had a neoclassical-style palace with two wings constructed here to serve as a resting-place on her journeys. In the center of the kremlin area is the grandiose monument unveiled in 1862 to mark the first millennium of Russian history featuring an angel blessing a kneeling woman.

The severe damage inflicted during World War II upon The Church of the Transfiguration of Christ in Kovalyovo, the Zehnt Monastery, and the Church of Our Savior at Nerediza has been largely repaired. Only a small portion of the exceptionally beautiful frescoes was saved. Little likewise remained of the historic buildings which represented the town's glorious past as a center of trade, a past which present-day Novgorod is fond of citing.

Novgorod's kremlin has always protected the town from destruction (upper left).

The kremlin walls and large sections of the fortifications have been beautifully restored (upper right).

The bell tower inside the kremlin is one of the town's main landmarks (right).

These wooden churches are among the best preserved cultural monuments (right, opposite).

Orient and Occident

There is good reason why **KAZAN** is praised as the pearl of the Volga. This 1,000-year-old town is a fascinating center of Islam in Russia—and a treasure trove of valuable architectural monuments

LOCATION:
Capital of the Tartarstan Republic on the Volga

BEST TIME TO VISIT:
All year round

GETTING THERE:
By train from Moscow

The new Kazan mosque, completed in time for the town's millennium celebrations, is the largest mosque in Europe (right).

Ivan the Terrible had the mighty kremlin constructed in the 16th century. Its surrounding walls are 16ft (5m) thick (below).

Of all the towns on the Volga, 1,000-year-old Kazan justifiably deserves the term "architectural pearl": it is the center of Islam in Russia and represents a fascinating combination of East and West. The present-day capital of the autonomous Republic of Tatarstan was founded in the 10th century by the Volga Bulgars. They merged 200 years later with the Mongols to become the legendary and mighty Golden Horde. Their princes, the Khans, lived in the Khanate of Astrakhan, the Crimea and Kazan.

Conquest by Ivan
Devoted to their Islamic-Sunnite faith since time immemorial, the Tatars were able to preserve their religious and cultural identity throughout the centuries. In 1552, Ivan IV, the Terrible, finally succeeded, after several attempts, in capturing the Khanate of Kazan, the first non-Russian town, and incorporating it into his empire. It was this triumphant victory which inspired the building of St Basil's Cathedral in Moscow's Red Square.

The kremlin is a World Heritage site
Ivan destroyed many ancient Tatar buildings in Kazan and had a kremlin constructed which is now on the list of World Heritage sites. With its limestone wall, measuring 16ft (5m) thick and fortified by 13 towers, it forms the historic core of Kazan. Situated in the center of the kremlin are

the Cathedral of the Annunciation, the Tainitskaya Palace and the Governor's House, now the seat of the President of Tatarstan.

Kazan's most conspicuous landmark is its 187-ft (57-m) high Suyumbika Tower. Legend has it that Ivan IV built it for a beautiful Tatar princess by that name whose hand he wanted to win. The tilting tower was allegedly built in just seven days. When Suyumbika looked over the parapet across her wonderful land she decided not to accompany the Tsar to Moscow, preferring to commit suicide instead.

Fight for self-determination
The Cathedral of Peter and Paul was built around 1720 during the period of Christianization under Peter I. At the same time, new mosques were also being built in the town. Despite all the attempts over the centuries to suppress them, the inhabitants of Kazan have repeatedly tried to regain their right to self-determination.

In 1992, they finally gained autonomy over a region numbering 3.7 million people. Around one million of these live in Kazan—most of them are Tatars and Russians, yet Catholics, Protestants, Jews and members of other religious minorities have also been absorbed here without difficulty. The Kazan Metro system began operation to coincide with the celebrations marking the city's millennium. Europe's largest mosque was also inaugurated at the same time.

These representative palace residences, which were built in the center of Kazan during the 19th century, now house luxury businesses (above).

One of the 13 fortified towers, which were built to defend the kremlin (left).

Ural cultural center

EKATERINBURG, on the frontier between Europe and Asia, is a modern metropolis

LOCATION:
Russia's fourth largest town in the Urals, 25 miles (40km) from the imaginary border between Europe and Asia

FOUNDED:
In 1723 by Vassily Tatishchev

SIZE:
Approximately 1.3 million inhabitants

The legendary writer, Maxim Gorky, and the notorious monk, Rasputin, both spent their boyhood here. However, Ekaterinburg is indelibly associated with a massacre that continued to engage people's emotions throughout the 20th century. It was here in 1918 that Nicholas II, the last Tsar, was executed, together with his entire family, by the Bolsheviks. However, Ekaterinburg, which was officially founded in 1723, deserves far more in terms of recognition than being remembered only for this one tragic event.

Center of iron manufacturing

Ekaterinburg, the fourth largest town in the Russian Federation numbering over 1.3 million inhabitants, has a tempestuous history. As early as the 11th century, this region in the central Urals, in which the town is situated, was the target for invasion by armies of the Principality of Novgorod.

Lying just a few miles from the imaginary boundary between Europe and Asia, Ekaterinburg quickly developed into an industrial center. The first iron mines were established here in the 17th century. As a result, the town grew rapidly into an important center in this part of the Tsar's empire. One by one, it acquired a university, a theater, an opera house and a large number of museums.

Its darkest hour came in July 1918 when the Tsar's family was murdered. A telegram, sent by Jakov Sverdlov, an influential politician, contained instructions ordering the execution of the Imperial family. Six years after this brutal execution, the town was even renamed Sverdlovsk in honor of the Tsar's murderer. It was not until 1991 that a decision was made to revert to its historical name of Ekaterinburg.

The city developed into one of the biggest industrial, cultural and economic centers in the Soviet Union. Its importance to the Communist regime is reflected in the fact that it was selected for the site of the bunker for the Soviet Union's "interim government."

One of the city's most famous sons is former Russian President Boris Yeltsin, who studied at the local

Polytechnic and took his first political steps toward a career in the Communist Party in the region.

Beautiful buildings

In the 18th century, the town still consisted of predominantly wooden buildings. Only the main administrative buildings were constructed of stone in those days, for example the mining companies' headquarters, which today houses the seat of the Urals Conservatoire.

During the late 18th and early 19th centuries, the town acquired numerous Classical-style buildings. The most impressive architectural masterpieces can be found around the square on Voznesenskaya Hill, which includes an extensive park. Other impressive architectural highlights include the Main Post Office, and the Uralski Rabochi (Workers of the Urals) publishing house. The town's most distinctive modern landmark is its huge television tower, which is still awaiting completion. Ekaterinburg, with its 1.3 million inhabitants, is a hub of economic and cultural life.

A red and white diamond pattern gives the roof of this building next to the railway station a jolly appearance (opposite).

Rotundas along the artificial waterways adorn the Acropolis Park, which provides a pleasant contrast to the hectic bustle of Ekaterinburg city with its 1.3 million inhabitants (above).

Flight of steps in Acropolis Park (left).

A church in memory of the Tsar

On July 17th, 1918, the last Tsar and his family were murdered by the Bolsheviks. The Church-on-the-Blood is a reminder of **EKATERINBURG'S** darkest hour

LOCATION:
Fourth largest Russian city 25 miles (40km) from the imaginary dividing line between Europe and Asia

FOUNDED:
In 1723 by Vassily Tatishchev

SIZE:
Approximatly 1.3 million inhabitants

The Church-on-the-Blood was built in memory of the last Tsar of Russia, Nicholas II, and his family, who were murdered in Ekaterinburg in the summer of 1918.

Supporters of the Russian Tsars still exist and actually comprise a large community. Even 100 years after the end of Imperial rule, they still yearn for a monarch, who, like Peter the Great, would lead Russia to a new and glorious future.

Nostalgic view of the past
Although they form a minority in terms of practical politics, the present-day Tsarists, who deliberately set themselves up in counterpoint to those in power in the Kremlin, are more popular than many imagine. Their nostalgic interpretation of the past and their vision of a strong leader have met with an enthusiastic response primarily on the part of those who were disadvantaged either under the Soviets or by current economic policy in Russia.

Their Mecca is Ekaterinburg where the Church-on-the-Blood stands on the site where the last Tsar, Nicholas II, and his family were murdered on July 17, 1918.

Shot and buried
For many years, the exact circumstances surrounding the execution have continued to give rise to speculation. What is known for certain is that the Tsar's family was arrested initially in Alexander Palace in Tsarskoye Selo. Nicholas II, his wife and children, as well as their entire staff of servants were then deported to Ekaterinburg. On the orders of Bolshevik leader Yakov Sverdlov, the last of the Romanovs were held prisoner in Ipatiev House, where they were eventually shot dead in the basement and their bodies later buried.

The wrong daughter
It remained a mystery for many years whether or not one of the Tsar's daughters had survived the massacre. Since the 1920s, a woman who turned up in Berlin, had claimed to be Anastasia. Although she did not speak any Russian, even people close to the Tsar's family believed her story. Several movies on the subject helped to feed people's imagination. When Anna Anderson, as she called herself, died of natural causes in 1984, DNA tests proved that she was not a member of the Romanov family, but a Polish woman called Franziska Schankowska.

Exhaustive investigations of the corpses from Ipatiev House have led to the conclusion that all the members of the family met their death here.

Final resting place in St Petersburg
The Tsars' story did not, as it happens, end there as the Bolsheviks hoped.

Eighty years later, the remains of the Tsar's family—with the exception of Alexey, the heir to the throne, and Maria, the Tsar's daughter, whose bodies could not be found—were transferred to St Petersburg. Tsar Nicholas and the last family of Romanovs were given a state funeral and laid to rest in the Peter and Paul Fortress in St. Petersburg.

Ironically, it was Boris Yeltsin who prepared the political ground for this to happen. In his capacity as Ekaterinburg's Party Secretary during the

1970s, it was he who was responsible for the demolition of Ipatiev House.

A new church was erected in its place in 2003: Church-on-the-Blood, also known as Savior-on-the-Blood Church. Majestically crowning a hilltop site, the building was constructed in the style of traditional Old Russian cathedrals. It is far more than just a church—it represents an apology in stone by modern Russia for the murder of the Romanovs.

Relics of sacred splendor

The Soviets destroyed many churches in **EKATERINBURG**, but the remaining six churches feature magnificent ecclesiastical architecture

LOCATION:
Fourth largest Russian city in the Urals, 25 miles (40km) from the imaginary dividing line between Europe and Asia

FOUNDED:
In 1723 by Vassily Tatishchev

SIZE:
Approximately 1.3 million inhabitants

Five golden cupolas adorn the roof of the Chapel of the Holy Martyr of St. Catherine (above, right).

Although the Cathedral of Ekaterinburg no longer exists, its bell tower still towers 180ft (5m) in height (above).

Ekaterinburg once boasted around four dozen churches—a considerable number of sacred architectural masterpieces which gave the town a most picturesque appearance

Soviet orgy of destruction

Following their Revolutionary victory, the Communist rulers began taking measures against the Russian Orthodox Church. Nowhere were these measures more radical than in Ekaterinburg. During the 1930s, the new rulers razed nearly all the churches. Any form of relic, which might remind people of a past the rulers sought to erase, was to be destroyed without trace.

Around half a dozen churches managed to survive this orgy of destruction on the part of the Soviets, including the most famous church of all, the Voznesenskaya Church, which was built in the 19th century.

The small "mining office headquarters" is a building dating from the 18th century. Situated away from the center, the Holy Trinity Cathedral, where Grigori Yefimovich Rasputin once spent some time as a monk, also survived destruction. Opposite this church, which gradually fell into disrepair, is the new Church-on-the-Blood, which was built as a memorial to the Tsar and his family, who were murdered in Ekaterinburg.

The imposingly large Alexander Nevsky Church, named after the legendary Novgorod prince, was also left untouched by the Bolsheviks.

The historical figure of Prince Nevsky, who liberated Russia from the Tatars, played an important role in the run-up to the outbreak of World War II. This national hero was borrowed to further the cause of Stalinist ideology. His name was invoked to mobilize people into defending the motherland.

Other churches that survived alongside the Church of St John the

Baptist were the Ascension Church and the Church of the Martyr St Catherine, who did after all give the town her name. She was regarded as the patron saint of miners.

This church represents something of a curiosity for while the regime had banned religious services in the remaining churches, the Church of the Holy Martyr remained open for worship throughout the whole of the Soviet era. No one was prevented from praying there. The reason for this exception was never discovered. It was possibly due to the fact that the church contains a precious icon, which is reputed to perform miracles.

No matter how many churches were destroyed by the Soviets, they did not succeed in achieving their professed goal of destroying the Russian Orthodox faith. On the contrary, even in Ekaterinburg, the Christian church remains very active to this day, with regular services being held in all the churches. A growing number of young people, especially, are embracing the Orthodox religion.

The Cathedral of John the Baptist is topped with onion-shaped domes decorated with stars (left).

Built in the Classical style and decorated with a gilded dome, the Holy Trinity Cathedral contrasts sharply with modern Ekaterinburg (below).

A city with Siberian flair

TOMSK boasts ornately decorated wooden buildings and is now a forward-looking university town

LOCATION:
Siberia, Tomsk region

BEST TIME TO VISIT:
May to September

GETTING THERE:
By air from Moscow

Small snowflakes have been gently falling, followed by a brief shower of rain, when, without warning, the warm season makes its appearance. The Siberian people have been familiar with their temperamental climate since time immemorial. They have adjusted to the fact that their vast region spends nine months of the year buried beneath a solid layer of snow and that summer ends in August after a few brief days of warmth.

The people's closeness to the soil in their harsh land is legendary. And this is particularly evident in Tomsk, a town that was originally established under a decree by Tsar Boris Godunov in 1604. It began life as a fortress citadel on the shores of the River Tom.

Success of the transport route

The building of the famous transportation route, known as the Great Siberian Tract, led to Tomsk's rapid development as a center of commerce during the two centuries that followed. The town's prosperity continued until 1830 and when gold was

discovered in the area Tomsk took on the character of a gold rush town.

The advent of the Trans-Siberian Railroad resulted in Tomsk, which numbers half a million inhabitants, losing its role as the region's principal town. The government in St Petersburg decided that the route of the track would cross a river bridge several hundred miles south of Tomsk, a decision which also heralded the birth of Novosibirsk. Tomsk was only connected to the legendary Trans-Siberian Railroad by a branch line and did not regain its significance

until World War II. As the German army was advancing on Moscow, the government together with around 30 crucial factories from the European part of the Soviet Union were evacuated to Tomsk. During the Cold War, numerous factories in Tomsk supplied materials to the Red Army.

Secret city

Foreigners were not welcome in Tomsk. In 1949, a secret town, codenamed "Post Box 5" and known as "Tomsk 7," was established a short distance from the main town. It became the site of a nuclear power plant.

It was not until 1970 that people rediscovered Tomsk's significance as an ancient town—at least by Siberian standards. Tomsk was designated a historic town and became famous for its wooden architecture, examples of which can be seen in the ornamental carvings decorating many of the villas and commercial buildings.

Tomsk possesses one of the oldest libraries in Siberia as well as stone-built churches. The most important church is the Peter and Paul Cathedral. The town also acquired a Roman Catholic Polish church. Islam is likewise represented and the town has its own mosque.

Nowadays, Tomsk is a forward-looking university town, renowned for its engineering, its timber-processing plants and chemical industry. The town has had its own airport since 1967 and the M 53 "Baikal" road from Novosibirsk to Irkutsk passes through Tomsk.

The first churches in Tomsk were built of wood and several stone churches were built at a later date. The Epiphany Cathedral was constructed in the 19th century (above, far left).

Siberia's first university was opened in Tomsk in the 19th century (above, left).

Façade decoration on a public building dating from the days of socialist realism (above, right).

Wood has always played a central role in house construction in Tomsk. This passageway demonstrates the excellence of the craftsmen's skill (left).

Nizhny Novgorod, the largest town on the Volga, was once an important trade fair center. From 1932 to 1991, it was known as "Gorky" after the writer Maxim Gorky and became a major producer of armaments (right).

Its most impressive architectural achievements include the Church of Our Lady of Smolensk and Vladimir, built in the 17th-century Stroganov Baroque style (opposite).

Culture at every turn

Over 600 historic and cultural monuments assure **NIZHNY NOVGOROD** of its place on UNESCO's list of World Heritage sites

Moscow
Nizhny-Novgorod

Russia

LOCATION:
Nizhny Novgorod region

BEST TIME TO VISIT:
Between May and September

GETTING THERE:
By train from Moscow

This city, regally put above all east of Russia, has absolutely whirled our heads. Its ravishing vast expanses are breathtaking to marvel at!" remarked the renowned painter Ilya Repin (1844–1930). This probably expresses what most people feel when they arrive in Nizhny Novgorod.

No other city outside the Tsarist strongholds of Moscow and St Petersburg has a greater cultural heritage than Nizhny Novgorod. This city on the Volga with its 1.4 million inhabitants is the fourth largest in the country.

Becoming a metropolis
Yuriy II, Grand Prince of Vladimir, founded the settlement in 1221. The town withstood the next 200 years of Tatar rule practically unscathed and established itself —thanks to its ambitious princes—as one of Russia's political centers.

During the 14th century, Nizhny Novgorod, as befitted the capital of the Principality of Suzdal, was provided with a mighty fortress complete with 13 towers and several cathedrals thanks to the ruling Grand Prince Dmitir Konstantinovich. He was consumed with an ambition to make his "Lower New Town," as its name translates, into a city as magnificent as Moscow.

This well-fortified town, which had meanwhile become part of Muscovy, went on to play a strategically important role in the struggle against the Tatars of Kazan. The mighty kremlin with its fortified towers was able to withstand several attacks. Around a hundred years later, a Nizhny Novgorod trader, Kuzma Minin, put together a volunteer army which, led by Prince Dmitry Pozharsky, succeeded in driving Polish forces out of Moscow.

The Stroganov School
Cultural development in Nizhny Novgorod reached a peak in the 17th century when the Stroganovs, one of the wealthiest Russian merchant families, settled in the town. They maintained their own art workshops, which employed some of the most prominent icon painters of the day. The style of icon-painting, which thrived under their patronage, became known in art history as "the Stroganov School."

This was not all, however; in the late 17th century the Stroganov family also donated money for Baroque churches. They built Virgin's Nativity Church—known as the "Stroganov Church" in honor of its sponsors— and the Church of Our Lady of Smolensk and Vladimir. Both are characterized by their unique architectural style.

The town subsequently developed into a thriving center of trade. Under the Soviets, who renamed the town "Gorky," it became a center for the arms industry and Mig fighter-interceptor jets are built here.

Nizhny Novgorod can be justifiably proud not only of its historical heritage, but also of its present-day cultural life. Several theaters and concert halls, 30 museums, various galleries and numerous cultural sites

await the visitor, including the private house of Andrei Sakharov, which is open to the public. Sakharov, a Nobel Peace Prize winner, was exiled to Gorky in 1980 after speaking out publicly against Russia's atomic weapons policy and the invasion of Afghanistan. Nowadays, the city's second most famous resident after Maxim Gorky has a festival of culture and music named after him.

The motherland's triumph

Europe's biggest statue stands on a hill above **VOLGOGRAD**, the city known as "Stalingrad" until 1961

LOCATION:
South Russian region of Volgograd

SPECIAL FEATURES:
Panorama Museum of the Battle of Stalingrad, Uliza Marshala Chuikova 2

GETTING THERE:
By train from Moscow

Invasions, sieges and destruction—the city of Volgograd has lived through many difficult times and is better known by its Soviet name of Stalingrad.

It originated with the foundation of a fortress in 1589 amid the steppes landscape along the shores of the River Volga, 250 mile (400km) north of the Caspian Sea. The fortification was intended as a defense against the nomadic tribes from the south and was named Tsaritsyn, which meant "yellow sand" in the Tatar language. Captured by Mongols and Tatars in the 17th and 18th centuries, Tsaritsyn was regarded as the headquarters of the Golden Horde.

Coal mining and oil production

Like all the towns on the Volga, Volgograd became an important center of trade with Rome, Constantinople and Greece. During the 19th century, coal mining and oil processing grew in importance. However, the deplorable living and working conditions of its people drove thousands of citizens toward revolution. Bitter fighting took place in Tsaritsyn during the civil war between 1917 and 1920 because of its strategic position at a junction of transport routes taking food supplies to Moscow and St Petersburg. In the end, Stalin's Red Army members inflicted a crushing defeat on the White Army troops of Tsaritsyn and renamed the town Stalingrad.

As such, it became renowned as the scene of one of the bloodiest battles of World War II. Hitler was determined to capture it in order to gain access to the oil supplies between the Caspian Sea and the Urals.

After weeks of fighting, by which time Stalingrad had been reduced to rubble, the counter offensive began. The German Army was ordered to stand its ground and as a result 200,000 Germans, 250,000 Russians and 300,000 civilians lost their lives.

Mother Russia

Situated on the crest of Mamayev Kurgan, a hill that was the scene of fierce fighting, is the "Mother Russia" memorial that commemorates the victims as well as the victory of Stalingrad. This 280-ft (85-m) high allegorical sculpture, the tallest in Europe, is a symbol of Soviet triumph and national pride. After the war, Stalingrad was awarded the status of "hero city."

It was rebuilt in accordance with the ideals of socialist state architecture. The city stretches for 37 miles (60km) along the river. Since 1961, its one million inhabitants have been allowed to call their city Volgograd again.

The "Mother Russia" monument on Mamayev Hill commemorates the victory over the German army. The sword alone measures 40ft (12m) in length (opposite).

Pure Soviet realism: a typical portrayal of a hero from the Stalinist era at the memorial to the Battle of Stalingrad (top).

View of the main section of the memorial, where wreaths are regularly laid (right).

Bastion of faith

PSKOV, a member of the Hanseatic League, boasted a democratic constitution, early on. It was also a popular place of pilgrimage

LOCATION:
In the northwest by Lake Pskov

BEST TIME TO VISIT:
May to September

GETTING THERE:
By train from St Petersburg

The westernmost town in Russia today is also one of the oldest. Founded by the Krivich tribe, its earliest recorded mention was in AD 903. Even then the town was referred to as "having existed a long time." For hundreds of years, Pskov, which eventually became a member of the Hanseatic League, functioned as a military outpost.

Independent principality

The process of Christianization began in the 10th century under Princess Olga, also known as St Olga. In the 13th century, Pskov became an independent principality. Its constitution, which guaranteed its people many freedoms, was exceptional for those days. The *veche*, or people's assembly, was comprised of merchants and artisans who had a major say in political decision-making.

The independent city-state was spared invasion by the Tatars, but its advantageous position attracted other enemies. Pskov adhered politically to Novgorod and was responsible for defending the frontiers and maintaining and extending its fortifications. Among the most persistent enemies were the Teutonic Knights, who were finally defeated by Alexander Nevsky in 1242 at the Battle of Peipus. The Prince of Novgorod had already been elevated to the status of national hero two years earlier when he defeated Sweden.

Appetite for invasion

Lithuania and Poland also made repeated attempts to conquer Pskov. During the 15th century, 16 separate attacks were successfully repelled. During this period, thriving trade relations developed between Russian and German merchants within the Hanseatic League, and art and religious life simultaneously flourished within the numerous monasteries.

In 1510, Pskov was incorporated into the Principality of Muscovy and although it was expanded 200 years later by Peter I, it nevertheless began to dwindle in importance.

During World War II, the town suffered heavy losses. Many of the surrounding villages were completely destroyed. Around 300,000 people lost their lives in the German attacks and many were driven away. Under Soviet rule, many important monasteries were either closed or destroyed.

The fortified walls of Pskov's kremlin bear testimony to the town's role as a military outpost (left and opposite).

These priory churches with their many additions are typical of Pskov (below, left).

The Trinity Church in the kremlin was substantially altered in the 17th century (below).

Unique architectural style

Pskov, once the hometown of Alexander Pushkin, has only really come alive again since perestroika. The imposing, medieval creations of Pskov's master builders and icon painters have been restored to fresh splendor.

The mighty kremlin complex, which includes the Trinity Church, dating from the 15th century, has been well preserved. The fortress is surrounded by walls fortified with towers.

The most important church in the Mirozhsky Monastery is the 12th-century Cathedral of the Transfiguration of Christ the Savior. A large number of smaller priory churches were also built around this time, along with the bell-walls, for which Pskov is renowned. It was not long before Pskov developed its own style of architecture and broke away from the model of Novgorod.

This town of 200,000 inhabitants, situated between St Petersburg and Latvia, is once again beginning to regain its former role as a popular center of pilgrimage.

The heart of Russia

Tiny St Nicholas Chapel in **NOVOSIBIRSK** once
marked the heart of the Tsar's empire

LOCATION:
In the region of
Novosibirsk on the
River Ob

BEST TIME TO VISIT:
May to September

GETTING THERE
Flights from Moscow

St Nicholas Chapel in Novosibirsk, small and inconspicuous, yet situated in a very prominent position, was constructed here in the heart of Siberia at the end of the 19th century to indicate the geographic center of the Tsar's empire.

The Russian borders have altered several times since then, yet Novosibirsk has remained at the heart of cultural and economic life in Siberia. It is often referred to as the "capital of Siberia."

From village to metropolis

By the end of the 19th century, it was still little more than a village in the vast taiga landscape. Within a few decades, however, Novosibirsk, formerly known as "Novonikolayevsk," had risen to become the most influential town in Siberia. This was due to the construction, one hundred years ago, of a bridge over the Ob river, which was destined to carry a section of the Trans-Siberian Railroad. The historic railroad building, one of the city's main sights, and the great bridge have become the most symbolic buildings in the metropolis, which now numbers 1.4 million inhabitants.

Since it was only founded relatively recently, the city does not have many historic buildings. The most important of its few churches is the Alexander Nevsky Cathedral, built in 1894 and one of the largest churches in this part of Siberia. Of particular note is the large and impressive Opera House, which is at the cultural heart of this fairly affluent town.

The city is highly regarded as an academic center. Situated at the most important transport intersection this side of the Urals, the town was a key center of research during the Soviet era—so much so that a settlement called "Akademgorodok" (Academics'

town) was artificially created. Up until a few years ago, this community remained tightly sealed off from the outside world.

Elite research center

This settlement was reserved for the country's greatest scientific brains. Economic shortages, which were a feature of the Socialist economy elsewhere in the country, were unknown on this "island of the fortunate" and the shops in Akademgorodok were always well stocked. The scientists enjoyed—what was by Soviet standards—a comfortable lifestyle with their families. They were employed by the military industrial complex and earned monthly incomes that were well above the national average. Today there are still three academies, 43 academic research institutes and over a hundred individual research centers.

The entire administrative region, which extends over an area of 193 square miles (500km^2), benefits from this center. Some of the financial investments flowing rapidly into Russia nowadays will also go to Novosibirsk. Thanks to the establishment of new manufacturing plants, the unemployment rate is considerably lower here than anywhere else in the Federation. Cultural life also flourishes.

The Opera House makes an important contribution to Novosibirsk's cultural life (above, left).

St Nicholas Chapel, in the center of the city, has been carefully renovated (above).

The Alexander Nevsky Cathedral has also been restored (left).

An Eastern air

Mosques and churches are reminders of the different cultures that made **ASTRAKHAN** an important trading center

LOCATION:
In southern Russia in the Astrakhan region

BEST TIME TO VISIT:
May to October

GETTING THERE:
Rail links and flights from Moscow

The very name of the town has an exotic ring to it and awakens associations with the Orient, stirring up visions of glowing Persian fabrics and conjuring up the scent of exotic spices and perfumes. The town lives up to its name, having, over the centuries, absorbed the influences of many cultures within its walls. Situated in the delta of the Volga, Astrakhan, like St Petersburg, is built on a collection of islands, all linked to each other by bridges. This is the point where the great Volga River flows into the Caspian Sea. Astrakhan now numbers 500,000 citizens and is still a busy port, which trades with Europe as well as the states bordering on the Caspian Sea.

Seat of a Tatar khanate

Thanks to its geographical situation, this seaport has, since the 6th century, been a center for the shipment of goods from the Middle East and southwest Asia. From here, merchant ships set sail for India and China and also headed westward toward European destinations. People and goods from all over the world came together in Astrakhan, left their mark, and gave the city its unique atmosphere.

Occupied by the Tatars in the 13th century, it was once regarded as the

Assumption Cathedral is at the heart of the Astrakhan kremlin. This two-story church, designed in Byzantine style, stands on a raised plateau and boasts five cupolas. Its present appearance dates from the early 18th century (left).

Astrakhan is the last Volga port before the Caspian Sea and is situated approximately 932 miles (1,500 km) from Moscow (bottom left).

capital city of the Golden Horde—the lost city of Sarai.

Exhibitions in the Tatar Museum recall this period and the White and Black Mosques also reflect the exotic atmosphere of the city.

In 1554, Astrakhan became part of the Russian Empire, but it did not begin to flourish until the era of Peter the Great. The White Kremlin with its five-domed Trinity Cathedral and Assumption Cathedral was built in the early 18th century. The master builder of the church, which was finished in 1698, was a serf. In addition to buildings designed in the style of Russian Baroque, the town also contains architectural monuments finished in the pseudo-Moorish, Classical and early Renaissance style. Merchants' houses, numerous churches and mosques bear testimony to Astrakhan's turbulent past. Of particular note is the Persian mosque, completed in 1859. The World War II museum serves to illustrate a dark chapter in the city's history.

National romantic works

Another exhibition is devoted to a native painter, Boris Kustodiev (1878–1927). He created romantic works based on Russian themes, painted in vibrant and intense colors.

Journey to the forbidden city

After World War II, **SAMARA** became an important arms production center, but is now open to visitors once more

LOCATION:
Samara region, on the Volga

BEST TIME TO VISIT:
May to September

GETTING THERE:
By rail from Moscow

According to an old folk song, the most beautiful girls in Russia come from Samara. This was possibly one of the reasons why many prominent artists settled there. Maxim Gorky got his first job with the Samara newspaper, Ilya Repin lived and worked in the city, and Leo Tolstoy bought himself a country estate here. But it was assuredly not just the beautiful women of Samara who inspired the painters and writers; it was also the magnificent surroundings and the famous town itself.

From Venice to the Volga

The small Samara river discharges here and gave the settlement its name. Eventually, Venetian merchants found their way here. As was the case in Volgograd, a small fortress was built here in 1590 as a defense against the invading forces from the steppes. Despite this, the Tatar army under Stepan Razin launched a successful attack in 1670 and captured the settlement. Two peasant uprisings were also launched from this town.

In addition to its lively trade in colonial goods, Samara also gained significance during the 19th century as the Russian Empire's most important wheat-growing and grain-processing center.

Renamed after Kuybychev, one of Stalin's closest comrades, the city was made a secondary capital in 1941, a fall-back base in the event that Moscow was occupied by the German Army. Before the battle for Moscow, the diplomatic corps and the entire military administration were evacuated here. Stalin's bunker is now a museum.

A closed city

Until 1991, the city remained a prohibited area. Neither Soviet citizens nor visitors were allowed to visit this arms production center. The town has now reverted to its old name of Samara and is renowned not only for its major industrial plants, but also for several famous universities. Samara also has a great deal to offer in cultural terms—it has four theaters and numerous exhibitions displaying valuable collections, including the popular State Museum of Space Travel.

Only a small part of its architectural heritage has survived. Several neo-Classical-style residences and Art Nouveau buildings serve as reminders of Samara's heyday, which came as a result of its prominence as an agricultural center.

The Monument to the Workers of the Air and Space Travel Industry dominates Glory Square in Samara (right).

Only a few of the original 40 historic churches have survived in Samara. The Cathedral of Samara, dedicated in 2006, is a memorial in honor of St George the Bringer of Victory (left).

Group of figures in a frieze decorating the Samara opera house, one of the city's main cultural centers (below).

One of the most popular leisure pursuits among the men of Sotchi is undoubtedly the fishing expeditions along the shore (above).

View of Sochi's passenger harbor (right).

Sochi has always been Russia's favorite spa. Shady walkways are inviting during the summer (opposite).

Mountain climbers get their money's worth in the Caucasus Mountains near Sochi (far right).